Haunted Missouri

haunted
missouri

A Ghostly Guide to the Show-Me State's
Most Spirited Spots

jason offutt

TRUMAN STATE UNIVERSITY PRESS

All photography by author, unless otherwise noted.
Cover photo: Lemp Mansion, third floor hallway (glow on lightbulb has been added)
Cover design: Teresa Wheeler

Type: Text is Minion Pro, Adobe Systems, Inc; display is Galahad, Adobe Systems, Inc.
Printed by: Thomson-Shore, Dexter, Michigan USA

Library of Congress Cataloging-in-Publication Data

Offutt, Jason, 1965–.
Haunted Missouri : a ghostly guide to the Show-Me State's most spirited spots / by Jason Offutt.
    p. cm.
ISBN 978-1-931112-66-6 (pbk. : alk. paper)
1. Ghosts—Missouri. 2. Haunted places—Missouri. I. Title.
BF1472.U6O37 2007
133.109778—dc22

2007009856

For all the kind souls who pointed me in the right direction while I researched this book. And for my wife, Kimberly, who put up with me traipsing around dark, spooky places for the past year, even though it gave her the heebie-jeebies.

Contents

Ghostly Graveyards

Returning to their Old Haunts

Someone's Watching You

Foreword

I'm a writer and a ghost hunter. As a card-carrying member of both semi-professions (check my wallet, I dare you), I would like to clear up some misconceptions. First, writing is not a glamorous business. Oh, sure, it sounds glamorous: throw together three hundred pages worth of boy-meets-girl, boy-loses-girl, boy-saves-planet-from-space-aliens; sign a few autographs; complain your back hurts from lugging all those royalty checks to the bank; and hang out with rock stars. However, it usually doesn't work like that.

With fiction writing, you spend hours a day stringing together thousands of words you're convinced are clever, only to wake up the next morning to find out they're not. You smell like you haven't bathed in days because you haven't and, by the way, you've got a hangover. With nonfiction writing, you spend just as much time writing and not bathing, but three times as much time researching, interviewing, driving enough miles to warrant an oil change between each trip, and writing out checks to credit card companies to pay for it all. And if the royalty checks really were big enough to hurt your back, there would be writer groupies, which there aren't... darn it.

Ghost hunting isn't glamorous either. It mainly consists of finding people who will actually talk about their encounter, fielding rejections from the majority of witnesses who won't, and loitering in deserted, remote, dusty, and usually creepy places waiting for something to happen. And how often do you think something happens? Not often. Ghosts are spiteful like that.

So why do writers and ghost hunters do it? Well, first, we have very understanding spouses. Thank you, honey. Second, most of us are nuts. We love writing and investigating because both processes are about discovering the unknown. Do ghosts exist? What was that cold spot? Will I make deadline? How do you spell noncorporeal? You see the allure, don't you?

Haunted Missouri: A Ghostly Guide to the Show-Me State's Most Spirited Spots took me a year and a half to write. This is partly because I have a day job, but mostly because it's a nonfiction book, and nonfiction books take time—lots and lots of time. The hundreds of interviews in this book were conducted between January 2004 and February 2007. Most interviews were conducted in person, but some were done over the telephone. Although most of the book took a year and a half to write, interviews for the following chapters were done in 2004: the Vaile Mansion, the Lemp Mansion, Big

Cedar Lodge, Senior Hall, the Elms Resort Hotel, and the Hotel Savoy. I interviewed owners or managers of haunted sites, eyewitnesses they recommended, historians, and ghost hunters. I visited and photographed each of these haunted spots and tried to get a good feel for the area's history. And, in doing so, I made a couple of trips around the whole state. Missouri is much bigger than it looks on a map. Trust me. I also experienced a few weird things along the way, but you'll have to finish the book to find out what those were.

There are thousands of haunted spots in Missouri, so I had to be picky. Each haunted place I investigated needed to meet two criteria to be included in this book: 1) It had to have some historic significance to Missouri. A haunted house is just a haunted house. But a house haunted by the ghost of Jesse James, well, that's something special; and 2) It had to be open to the public because I want you to be able to visit and experience the history and, hopefully, the ghosts. I found these locations through research in libraries and archives, interviewing local experts in folklore, talking to people who work or live in historic and "haunted" places (the creepier the better), and through tips from friends, fellow ghost hunters, and strangers who have experienced the paranormal. After that, I weeded out the unreliable, the attention-seeking, and the weird guy who gets e-mails from Jesus. I'm serious and objective about the paranormal, so I only interviewed those who were also serious about the subject.

Missouri is rich in culture, history, fun, adventure, and some flat-out weirdness. I'd like you to go find out for yourself. This is *Haunted Missouri*. I hope you have as much fun with it as I did.

Jason Offutt
Maryville, Missouri

Ghost Hunting Basics

I have seen a ghost. At least, I think it was a ghost. I was ten years old, and ten-year-olds see a lot of things—especially in the dark. Things that, when Mom or Dad flip on the bedroom light, turn out to be lamp silhouettes, Little League trophies, Satan … the usual. But my ghost was in a hallway. A dim hallway, sure, but it was afternoon and enough sunlight crept through the shadows from both ends of the hall that it would have been pretty hard for me to mistake a coat rack for what I saw. I saw an eight-year-old boy. He was dressed in a flannel shirt and jeans, his hair was dark and tousled. He didn't smile. He didn't frown. He didn't say anything. He just looked at me and I just looked at—and through—him. Yeah, through. I could see the wall and part of a bookshelf through him. I didn't scream. I didn't run. I just turned and walked away, not looking back to see if the boy followed me, disappeared, or turned into something toothy and slathering like they showed on the Saturday afternoon movies.

When I was brave enough to come out of my room and look down that hallway, he was gone. I never told anyone about the little boy because I knew they wouldn't believe me. But I saw him. That's why I wrote this book. There are things we don't know about. Things that wander in and out of shadows in your home. Things that rattle doorknobs, move furniture, or open cabinets when no one is there. Things that can only be explained one way—you've been paid a visit by a ghost.

What is a ghost?

Before we go ghost hunting, let's look into the basics. First, what is a ghost? An unexplained magnetic field? The nonphysical remnant of the dead? Or just imagination? Candace Klemann of Hannibal is sensitive to the spirit world. She believes ghosts are spirits of the dead: "Hauntings exist because people leave their essence behind because something big happened." 'Big' being a murder, a suicide, or death from sickness or an accident—a death that may have taken the person by surprise. "Many ghost sightings are ghosts who don't know they're dead," she said.

Sally Rhine Feather, PhD, director of development of the Rhine Research Center at Duke University, said there's plenty of debate among parapsychologists as to what, exactly, this ghostly phenomenon may be. "I don't know if there is any one professional perspective," she said. "Some phenomena, like poltergeists, have been thought to be spontaneous PK [psychokinesis] unconsciously produced by repressed young people and possibly some haunting phenomena might even be the same thing." Haunting phenomena that peak during certain night hours, she said, could be triggered by subtle physical energies such as geological causes—as is suggested in the Missouri hauntings at Bone Hill in Levasy and Spook Light Road near Seneca. But some parapsychologists offer a more spiritual explanation. "Others believe that some type of consciousness exists beyond death and sort of remains in certain locations," Sally said. "Many afterdeath encounter reports in all cultures raise the possibility of spirit survival, especially in well-documented cases where apparitions of apparently departed people are seen by several people and/or animals with reactions. The only alternative to a spirit surviving other than fraud or misperception is some sort of group hallucination." But even with this evidence of spirits, is there scientific proof? Not really, but occasionally a psychic reading makes even scientists take notice. "Some studies have found mediums to pick out certain spots independently of field investigators and that helps suggest that something is there—is it a spirit, a type of energy, persistence of effect over time?" Sally said. Readings at the Lone Jack Battlefield and Pythian Castle come to mind.

Dawn Newlan, a medium with the Ozark Paranormal Society, can see earthbound spirits and classifies them into three types. "You have ghosts that are just ghosts. They're people who are gone and come back," she said. "You have negative energies like your poltergeist. Negative energies can be worked with and straightened out. And you can have things that are just evil and you'll know. It'll just kick your butt." Not everyone, however, can see a ghost. But it helps if you believe in them. "Some believe and some don't," Candace stated. "I suspect belief may keep the ghosts around." Belief may be an integral part of seeing a ghost and may also increase the impact of such a sighting, but just believing in ghosts doesn't mean you'll ever see one. "Some people can see and some don't," Candace said. "If you have a belief... you're more open to them. But it's almost like tuning a radio."

Betsy Belanger of St. Louis believes in ghosts. Heck, she even talks to them. Betsy, director of the St. Louis Spirit Search, directs ghost tours of one of the most haunted buildings in America, the Lemp Mansion in St. Louis, and communicates with ghosts there. The best way to have a ghostly experience, she said, is to hang around in dark places. "At that time your ability to see paranormal activity is enhanced because there's less light. It's a lot like looking at stars. It's the same principle. The lower the light, the better your opportunity is to see something. My best advice is to go in there and to wrap yourself in a positive frame of mind. Keep it lighthearted without making a joke of it. Always listen. Concentrate as quietly as you possibly can. Keep the lights low, if that's an option to you, and be respectful. If you combine all those things, you may encounter something."

Lee Prosser of Springfield calls himself a "sensitive." He has heard ghosts and seen ghosts, but he doesn't think experiencing the paranormal takes a special gift. "There's nothing being psychic about it at all. Everyone's got the ability to do it. You just have to get over some preconceived...notions and let yourself be aware. If you do that, you're going to be seeing and hearing what you anticipated." Lee, a columnist for the webzine www.ghostvillage. com, has written stories on the paranormal since 1963. Although he believes everyone can experience the paranormal, he knows why they do not. "Basically what happened, you just shut it down," he said. "You just simply say: I'm making a conscious decision right now. I'm not going to see or hear or talk to anything that's not here in the flesh and you do it. People do it every day."

Lee says even sensitives can shut down what they see and hear. "Sometimes if I open myself up to it, I do have the ability to feel a presence. Sometimes I see them and sometimes I do not. My gift is not perfect at all. You can't do it on demand. Most people can't." It is society, Lee said, that closes our mind to anything out of the ordinary. "Every kid has a little imaginary friend as they're growing up. They're not imaginary—they're spirits. But there's a time when parents say it's time to put away the toys and grow up. People don't talk about things for fear of ridicule of people thinking they're out of a Cracker Jack box."

Although it's fun to take someone ghost hunting with you, don't take too many people. Ghosts can be shy. "The only time the spirits aren't as prevalent," Betsy warns, "is when there are a lot of people there." Candace suggested using emotions to attract a ghost. "[Encounters] occur when the emotional content is high, most frequently. It doesn't matter what emotion it is." Of course, what do you do if you find a ghost? Faint? Run? Scream? "If you don't want them, you can tell them to leave," Candace said. "You have that power."

Lee takes it a little further. "If it's an unhappy spirit, just laugh like crazy," he said. "A lot of ghosts, not all, died under bad circumstances—depressing circumstances. That's one way to disperse them is laugh."

Uh, yeah. I'll try that.

Ghost Hunting Checklist

Before you head out to your local cemetery/hotel/abandoned hospital/historic battlefield to scare up a resident spirit, here are some basic rules of ghost hunting:

1. Take loads and loads of beer. No, no, wait. Scratch that. No beer, tequila shooters, recreational prescription drugs, cigarettes, and especially no chewing tobacco—it's nasty. Any sort of substance that alters your senses can ruin a good ghost hunt. I hope this clears things up—that was not Rule 1.

The Real Rule 1—not that stupid fake Rule 1. Not everything weird you experience will be a ghost. It could be crickets, the house settling, vibrations from a passing train, faulty equipment, or the fact that you're scared out of your wits. Keep your mind open to anything, but not everything.

2. Respect other people's property. No matter where you're conducting an investigation, you are someone's guest—whether that someone be a private property owner, the government, an organization, or the ghost itself. So be a welcomed guest—don't trespass, keep quiet, don't litter, don't break anything, and for God's sake, keep your pants on.

3. Visit the area in daylight first. Becoming familiar with the area—especially any obstacles you may trip over when you run screaming into the night—may save you a broken foot. Then you can go back in the dark with your bearings straight.

4. Let people know where you are. Ghost hunting itself is safe, but the areas may not be. Abandoned buildings can be dangerous places and, though a ghost probably can't hurt you, people can. If you are ghost hunting in a public place, let the police know you're going to be there. Bail can be expensive.

5. Don't always go alone. Besides the safety factor, a witness to back up your story would be nice.

6. Research the area and history of the haunting as best you can. Interviewing property owners, caretakers, and witnesses, and visiting libraries and archives can give you insight on how to conduct your investigation.

7. Take the right equipment. Such as:
   - The proper clothing. If it's cold, take a jacket. If you think you're going to be running for your life, wear tennis shoes. If it's Halloween, take a pillowcase for all the candy. Just use common sense.
   - A camera. Anything from a 35mm disposable camera to a digital camera will work. You just need to document your hunt and, hopefully, anything paranormal you may encounter. Even if you don't see anything, take a picture. You never know what might show up on film.
   - Film. This may sound silly, but it's not only frustrating to be in the middle of a ghost hunt and realize you are out of film, it's embarrassing. Even the ghosts will laugh at you. Use high-speed film, anything from 400 to 1600 speed, and take plenty of it.
   - Thermometer. Ghosts are associated with sudden cold spots. A thermometer can help you determine if there is actually a cold spot or if it's your imagination.
   - Compass. Not only will a compass react to electromagnetic fields associated with ghosts, getting lost in the woods is as embarrassing as forgetting the film.
   - A notebook and something to write with. Record everything, like time of day (bring a watch), temperature, what you saw, what you heard, what you felt, what you smelled, weather conditions, interviews, etc.
   - Flashlight. Ghost hunting is best in the dark. Seeing is best when you're walking. Don't forget the flashlight.
   - Batteries. Sometimes during a ghost hunt, batteries go dead for no apparent reason, so take plenty of backups.
   - Cell phone. You never know when you may need to call for help … or pizza.
   - Proper ID. Just in case you run into the police.
   - An open mind. "If you're more comfortable and you hear voices, just close your eyelids and listen," Lee said. "They may have a message for you."

Lastly, if, during the course of your ghost hunt, a deep, disembodied voice tells you to get out—do it. Candace said something may be watching you: "There's a lot going on that we can't see."

Map locators

1 1859 Jail, Marshal's Home, &
   Museum
2 Anderson House
3 Bone Hill
4 Fort Osage
5 Lone Jack Battlefield
6 Wilson's Creek National Battlefield
7 Kendrick House
8 Rockcliffe Mansion
9 Lemp Mansion
10 Vaile Mansion
11 Big Cedar Lodge
12 Grand Avenue Bed & Breakfast
13 1069 Salon & Spa
14 Mt. Gilead School
15 Roberta Hall
16 Senior Hall

17 Yeater Hall
18 Central Methodist University
19 Workman Chapel
20 Hazel Ridge Cemetery
21 Peace Church Cemetery
22 Glore Psychiatric Museum
23 Mark Twain Cave
24 The Elms Resort & Spa
25 Jesse James Farm
26 Governor's Mansion
27 Old Tavern
28 Spook Light
29 Pythian Castle
30 Landers Theatre
31 Hotel Savoy
32 Main Street Café

Remnants of War

War has left its mark on Missouri, from the bloody Civil War battles at Lexington, Lone Jack, and Wilson's Creek, to the frontier fighting watched from behind the roughly hewn walls of Sibley's Fort Osage. Some Missouri families, like those from Levasy and Carthage, left their homes in the night, abandoning their farms, their belongings, and sometimes their fortunes. Hate once raged through this state—a hate so fierce it may linger still.

Chapter 1

1859 Jail, Marshal's Home, and Museum

INDEPENDENCE

Rain danced off the Independence streets the morning I pulled up to the 1859 Jail, Marshal's Home, and Museum. The water-darkened red bricks of the rectangular building were dotted with green shutters that framed blackened windows. I was early. The museum was closed. The building, just off the city's historic square, was a Union stronghold in a Southern-sympathizing county during the Civil War. The marshal and his family lived in the friendly two-story brick structure visitors see when they pass by on the street. But the jail's limestone cells downstairs were home to criminals, Southerners, chain gangs, and, for a time, outlaw Frank James. Some people think a restless spirit still calls one of the cells home. I didn't stare

into the dark windows to see if a face was looking back. I should have, but I didn't know the windows had a story to tell. Not until later.

A bolt of lightning brightened up the dark gray sky as I waited for a sign of tour guide John Cianciolo. John had seen something in the 150-year-old jail, and I wanted to know what. The rain subsided enough for me to get out of my car to walk toward the building, but a man in a black cowboy hat waved me over to his car. It was John. His black boots, hat, and uniform of an Old West US marshal looked out of place behind the wheel of a twenty-first century horseless carriage. I sat in the passenger seat and asked John about ghosts. "I can only tell you what I know and I believe," he said, the black cowboy hat riding low on his head. "The rest has got to be up to you." We left his car and went inside the museum. Despite the rain beating on the roof, the air in the welcoming area of the museum was stifling hot. I began to sweat and wondered how John, in his heavy marshal's uniform, kept his composure. I guess he was used to it.

John started volunteering at the jail in early 1989, a few months after retiring as an electrician. It was then he heard stories of people on the street outside the jail and marshal's home seeing curtains move or the shadow of a man in the window. Not anything out of the ordinary, except that passers-by reported seeing these things after hours, when the museum was closed and the volunteers had gone for the day. Those volunteers have also seen the shadows moving in the windows as they left for home. John wasn't impressed by the stories—at the time. Nor was he impressed when a man claiming to be psychic held a séance in the jail. John took me from the museum welcoming area down to the cells. The lights that bathed the cell area in their yellow tungsten glow seemed as out of place in this old jail as John's uniform did in his car. Old iron doors were still mounted on the limestone walls, probably still capable of holding prisoners. In the 1800s, these doors were pulled shut behind those who committed crimes large and small.

"At that time people could go to jail for horse racing around the square," John explained. "No drinking, no gambling, no shooting. It's no wonder a lot of people got into covered wagons and headed west so they could have more fun." But what filled the cells was Order No. 11. During the Civil War, Order No. 11 required people in this Union-controlled pro-South area who lived more than five miles from a Union garrison to leave their homes, move to town, and swear allegiance to the Union or face arrest. That meant a lot of Southern sympathizers saw the walls of that jail—sometimes twenty-five to a

cell. The hardships from that era may have left an impression in the jail. John led me into the middle cell that now held only a striped blanket and a flat pillow. The heat so prevalent upstairs was gone from the jail area. The cold was not the pockets of cold air associated with a haunting, but was more like the dank coolness of a cave. "The guy who was psychic wouldn't go into this cell," John said. "But he put his arm in and all the hair on his arm stood up."

Did John believe the psychic had felt a restless spirit? "You might," he said, the corners of his mouth betraying a grin. "But I'm from Missouri. You've got to show me." But someone—or something—took on John's challenge. He was standing in the hall of the cell area one day when he realized the ghost stories surrounding the marshal's home and jail might be real. "My niece and my youngest daughter were in a cell here and I heard my name. And I fully expected to see [then-museum director] Gay Clemenson," he said, pointing down the hall toward what now is the museum. "What I saw was a shadow walk out of that doorway and walk into that cell." "That cell" was the one the psychic wouldn't enter. "As far as I'm concerned, that's where he lives." The blanket and pillow on the cold, hard floor of the cell are arranged as if someone were staying there—and maybe someone is. "They've [volunteers] come in in the morning and it's been messed up," John said. "Like someone had slept there."

But the jail cells aren't the only spots people have experienced the unexplainable. John led me to the marshal's home, my shoes slapping against the original hardwood floors walked on by lawmen, soldiers, politicians, and outlaws. A desk once owned by statesman Henry Clay sits in the marshal's office, as does a reprint of a painting by Independence artist George Caleb Bingham depicting the strife caused by Order No. 11. The home is decorated with furniture and art not originally from the marshal's home but from the period. As with anywhere in the home and museum, the jail cells aren't too far away. "If you're sitting in the front, it's not uncommon to hear the [cell] doors open and close," said Lindsey Gaston, development director at the Jackson County Historical Society. "There's some obvious sounds of metal hitting stone. Unfortunately, you get kind of used to it."

Some people have not been able to get used to the spirit of the jail. As John led me upstairs to the marshal's family bedrooms, he told me a former museum director experienced something on the second floor. Something that left a not-so-friendly impression on him. "It scared him so bad he wouldn't come up here after dark," John said. "But he wouldn't say what happened." Others have felt a ghostly presence on the second floor during John's tours. While in an upstairs bedroom, a man blurted out, "There's someone here. There's a spirit here." John could have been more comforting. "I said, 'Yes, he lives downstairs in a cell.' He broke out in a real cold sweat. We had to get towels to dry him off."

But other than shadows, noises, and the occasional door creaking open on its own, there is something about the 1859 Jail, Marshal's Home, and Museum that tickles another sense. "About the second day I was over there in the back jailers' stairs, there was the very heavy aroma of cigar smoke," Lindsey said. "I thought it was just me and I mentioned it to someone and they gave me this smile and said, 'Yeah, that happens all the time.'" The building is on the National Register of Historic Places and is government property, so smoking is not allowed. So who's smoking in the building? One marshal died in a shootout at the jail. Although records do not show prisoners dying in the jail, John said the records are sketchy, so it's possible a prisoner died there and it was never included in the jail's history. The smoker could be the marshal, a prisoner, or somebody famous. "The smoke's in different rooms, but mostly in the sheriff's office," John explained. "They tell me Frank James smoked cigars. It may be him."

Frank James was never really a prisoner in the jail. John called him a "guest." Frank turned himself in and, while the Missouri governor was deciding his fate, stayed in a nicely furnished cell. He dined with the marshal's family and enjoyed being a celebrity. Oh, and Frank's cell was unlocked. Then could it be Frank James in the kitchen, too? "I was in the kitchen just a couple of weeks ago," Lindsey said. "I was sitting there filling in some time and I just started smelling it—fresh baked bread. I thought, 'That was interesting. There's not a bakery in the area.'"

Lindsay also revealed that certain pictures have moved from the walls overnight and a Christmas tree once put in Frank James's cell was inexplicably outside the cell the next day. "You feel like you're being watched," Lindsay said of the jail. "But a lot of people who've spent a lot of time there, they feel like they're being protected by them." John does. He's even experienced the spirit outside the jail.

"April 7, 1999, I had open-heart surgery at Research [Medical Center in Kansas City]," he told me. "Two orderlies came and said, 'We're going to take you to the operating room.' I saw a silhouette at my feet of a man with an orange glow. He was shaking his head up and down and I knew everything would be all right." He saw that same silhouette during another surgery March 18, 2000, at the Mayo Clinic, and has smelled the cigar smoke in his truck. "He's never scared me," John said. "He just lets you know he's here."

1859 Jail, Marshal's Home, and Museum

217 North Main Street, Independence, MO 64050

Phone: 816/252-1892
Website: http://www.jchs.org/jail/museum.html
Hours: March through October: 10 AM–4 PM Monday through Saturday, 1–4 PM Sunday
Tours: Group tours by appointment, includes student field trips.
Admission: adults $5; children 6 to 16 $2; seniors $4

Chapter 2

Anderson House, Battle of Lexington State Historic Site
LEXINGTON

Frozen grass crunched under my feet as I stepped outside the Battle of Lexington State Historic Site museum and onto the grounds of the Anderson House. When hemp mogul Oliver Anderson built the twenty-three-room house in 1853, a Lafayette County newspaper called it "the most sumptuous home west of Saint Louis, Missouri." I was anxious to see what 153 years and nineteenth-century artillery fire had done to the home that had been a pivotal landmark in the Civil War's Battle of Lexington. The three-story brick house sits 125 yards from the battlefield where lead bullets and cannonballs screamed through the air for three days in September 1861—some of them pointed at the Anderson House even though the Union Army used it as a hospital. The house changed hands three times during the battle, racking up about 120 Union, Confederate, and Missouri

State Guard casualties.

According to local ghost stories, some of the soldiers may not know the battle is over. "From people in the public, they've reported seeing soldiers on the battlefield," said Janae Fuller, resource manager with the Battle of Lexington State Historic Site. And she wasn't talking about reenactors—I asked. The ghostly experiences, however, aren't limited to Civil War soldiers. "Up in the southwest bedroom, they've heard a lady singing from a closet area," Janae explained. "There's also been supposedly a face that appears in the window of the southeast bedroom."

Although members of the staff have heard footsteps, hammering, and crying, an old-fashioned barred door convinced some of them that something about the Anderson House wasn't quite right. "One day, when staff were over there, apparently a bar just flew off the door without anybody being around it," Janae said. "Which is odd."

Frigid wind spat in my face as I followed my guide, Jan Henrikson, down the grassy path to the Anderson House through a backyard garden surrounded by a white wooden fence that looked dead and ghostly itself in the Missouri winter. The grounds of the Anderson House look much as they did when the home was built, the yard, entrenchments, and battlefield never falling under the plow. The L-shaped home is still impressive, a century and a half atoning for the three days of terror the house went through in the 1860s. We stepped onto the wooden slats of the porch that ran along the rear of the building and went inside. It was cold there too; the tall ceilings were meant for comfort in Missouri summers, not winters. A naked artificial Christmas tree sat next to a table in the foyer surrounded by plastic Wal-Mart sacks, a little out of place in a building that saw the deaths of smallpox victims and soldiers torn apart by primitive bullets.

"We're in the middle of redecorating," Janae said. I wasn't worried about decorations. I wanted ghosts, or at least a cold spot. In this weather, a cold spot might actually seem warm. She took me into a room that was once filled with screams, sobbing, and death. "This is the room where they say they set up a makeshift hospital," she said. A door atop two sawhorses sits in the middle of the room, like a temporary operating table might have looked in the 1800s. A display of 1860s medical equipment was spread over the door, complete with knives and saws doctors used to remove limbs too badly damaged to save. "I'm sure there was a lot of pain and misery," Janae said before we left for the house. She'd also told me what to look for.

"The blood stain in the fourth bedroom. It's a legend.... There was a lot of blood."

Three 145-year-old bloodstains dot the room's hardwood floor. For a place of pain and misery, the operating room is surprisingly quiet—a lot more quiet than the stairs. The staircase rises from the black and white-checkered floor of the foyer and spins up three flights. On this staircase, the tour guide for my third grade class field trip told us that Union soldiers pushed Confederates troops from the top of the stairs. If the Southern soldiers missed the Union bayonets thrust toward them and survived that whole gravity thing, they were free to go when they landed—if they could get up and walk away. That is what the guide said back in 1973, but the tour guides don't say that anymore.

It was a good story, but people have embellished the facts over the years. "The Southern soldiers were taken prisoner and were walking down the stairs," Janae said. "The Union soldiers with bayonets charged them. Then one soldier jumped over the stairs and escaped." The stairs were a little unnerving no matter the story, and I instinctively grabbed the banister when I neared the second floor. It was a long way up and it seemed an even longer way down. That's probably one of the reasons seasonal interpreter Christi Gonder doesn't like going too far up the stairs.

"The thing that probably unsettled me the most was the attic. We no longer allow people up there," Christi said. "It's kind of just creepy all around." However, I like attics. Yes, attics are creepy and dusty, good places to meet something spooky. Christi did. "I don't really like to go up there anyway," the Missouri State University agricultural communications major explained. "As I was going up there one day, I was walking up the stairs and I distinctly felt something grab my arm. I turned and there wasn't anyone there."

Janae and I stopped on the second floor landing. A sign reading "Closed" was draped over the stairs that led to the attic. "Do you want to see the attic?" she asked. I smiled, "Sure."

Original plaster from 1853 still covers the walls of the two-room attic, though the plaster has been chiseled with graffiti. During the 1960s and 70s, when the Anderson House wasn't as well cared for, vandals often visited the attic, probably with dates, and commemorated the night with their pocket knives. "That's what high school kids do," Janae said of the vandalism. "They even left their names."

A length of twine is pulled tight across one room of the attic, showing the trajectory of a cannonball that smashed through the house, a half-moon shape broken out of a support beam. The cannonball also left a shot-put sized hole in the ceiling of a second floor room, and some walls in the home are pockmarked with bullet holes. The three days in September 1861 were hot, Union troops had run out of water, there was no way to move their dead and dying, and people were shooting cannonballs at them. It was a miserable time to be Union in Missouri.

Maybe it still is, at least to whatever it was Christi heard. "I noticed up the back staircase to the servants quarters there was a door open. I went to shut it before any [visitor] got up there, but I got halfway up and I heard weeping and I heard running footsteps. At the point where they should have crossed where I could see them, I didn't see anyone, but I heard the footsteps continue on into the next room. I decided the door could stay open a little while longer."

Christi has heard stories of a cane flying across a room over a group of reenactors playing poker, ghostly children, and noises no one can explain. The sound-activated tape recorders put in the house have recorded noises during the night, "but it's normally trains that have set it off," she said. "I go back and forth from thinking it's an overactive imagination to maybe there is something. But the grabbing—I haven't been able to rationalize that one."

Although Janae's never experienced anything supernatural in the Anderson House, she's heard plenty of stories over the years, ones similar to Christi's. But one tour group from Jamaica took her by surprise. "They asked if I've ever had any experiences with ghosts or spirits, although it wasn't included in the tour, and I said no," Janae said. "But they said they felt vibes and the spirits were friendly."

As I left the house, I thought the spirits were a little too friendly during my visit, or at least too quiet for the site of a bloody Civil War battle. I could have been there at the wrong time of day, or maybe the ghosts just thought my ancestors fought on the right side. I walked back up the path by the garden toward the museum and offices, breath streaming from the corner of my mouth into the December afternoon, and I thought it would be fun to investigate the Anderson House again. But maybe in the summer.

Anderson House, Battle of Lexington State Historic Site

1300 John Shea Drive, Lexington, MO 64067

Phone: 660/259-4654
Website: www.mostateparks.com/lexington/
Anderson House Tours
Hours: March through October, 10 AM-4 PM Monday through Saturday; noon-6 PM Sunday; November through February by appointment only.
Admission: adults $2.50; students (6-12) $1.50; under 6 free

Chapter 3

Bone Hill

LEVASY

A great wooden cross looms over Ebenezer Church Cemetery. Past a grove of naked, bent trees at the foot of a blue-slope hill, the cross stands like a sentinel over the field-studded Missouri River valley. Farming is the industry in this part of Jackson County, and the striped fields, dead in the winter afternoon in silent reverence, and earth tones, stretch for miles beneath Bone Hill, the home of the cemetery, and the cross. The high hill has been revered for centuries—if you believe the stories. "One of the reasons people say it's Bone Hill is the Indians used to lay their buffalo bones out there and they would get bleached in the sun," said Jackson County historian Vicki Beck. Which, according to fellow historian Bob Wynn, who grew up in nearby Levasy, is an accepted story. Early settlers to the area, he said, found "arrowheads, flint scrapping tools, and bleached buffalo bones" on Bone Hill. The hill quickly

grew steep as I drove from the trees and made the half-mile approach to Bonehill Road. Although the view of the river valley stretched for miles, the cross dominated the landscape from as far as a half mile away. I was going to visit the cemetery, walk around the tombstones, and stand beneath the cross. I just hoped nothing was nailed to it.

"It's an incredible site," Vicki said of the peak of Bone Hill. "Supposedly for the Indians, it was a watch point for them. If you go out there and stand on that point, you can see five different counties." But Indians, buffaloes, and bones aren't the only story of Bone Hill. The legend behind the tombstone-studded hill is the seven-year light. "There's a story about the Civil War," Vicki said. "This fellow lived in the area and he buried his gold near the wall."

The man, whose name is lost to history, sold his farm in 1862, after he allegedly buried an undetermined amount of gold at the base of a stone fence built by slaves. The fence, made of the flat gray shale of the hill, stretches across a pasture to the north of the cemetery overgrown by bent trees and weeds, and is surrounded by dried cow patties. It can't be seen from the road, unless you know it's there. Whether the farmer anticipated trouble for South-ern sympathizers such as himself when the area fell under Order No. 11, or whether he was just lucky to sell his farm before his neighbors were forced to abandon theirs and flee is not known. But like many others, he left.

During the Civil War, a lot of people left. But before the farmer fled from Jackson County, he said he would come back in seven years to reclaim his gold. No one from his family came back, but seven years later, something did—a light that "puffs up like a glow and goes away," Bob said he'd been told by the late Edwin F. Borgman, who owned the property when Bob was a kid. Was it the farmer's ghost, searching for his lost gold? The first sighting was in 1869, seven years after the family left Jackson County. There were occasional sightings of the light during the early years, but over the last 40 years, sightings have been rare, though Bob has seen it—twice.

"When I was a kid—I was ten years old—I asked my mom that night, there was a bunch of boys with bikes," Bob said. "They were going to chase it down and my mom laughed and told me not to get onto the highway. I was more or less scared to death." Bob went with a group of older boys and what he saw has stuck with him since. "We just saw a glow and we tried to chase it down. It was a glowing spot we could see amongst the trees. We thought it was a prank." But they didn't catch it. So he and his friends tried again. "The second time we parked behind the stones at the woods," he said. "We were big enough then. We were going to jump out and tackle that sucker. Every time we did, it disappeared. It would be in front of us and all of a sudden be one hundred yards to the north. Ain't nobody gonna move that fast." The yellow light moved away from them, low to the ground. Bob and his friends chased it, but they never caught it. "The brush was pretty thick," he said. "We couldn't haul ass and surround it. We tried."

Vicki was also intimate with the reality of the light. Although she hasn't seen the light, her husband has. "My husband and his friends camped out there and he saw it too," she told me. "He was maybe fifteen. It was kind of cool for them to camp out there by the cemetery. They saw something and they packed up and left."

Vicki and Bob both said scientists have visited the site to investigate the light. They have pinned the phenomenon on the composition of the rocks. "Geologists went up there twenty years ago or more," Vicki said. "They took core samples and there are layers of shale in the ground on the hill. I guess it has something to do with the weather and gasses creep up through the shale." The shale is gassy? "They had some scientist out there," Bob said. "They thought some kind of shale. It has to be something like that."

Shale, snail, what about the gold? Neither Vicki nor Bob puts much stock in the gold theory. "Edwin Borgman [former landowner], he used to tell us kids about it all the time," Bob said. "He'd swear he could see the light but never got close to it. Every seven years he could see it. He never said it was a ghost and he never believed in the gold either." Vicki agrees: "It's a cool place. We've been up and down that rock wall with metal detectors."

The rock wall can be seen from the cemetery, pointing north toward Levasy, but a barbed-wire fence surrounding the pasture made it inaccessible—trespassing charges and possible jail time cuts down on ghost hunting. The fence can best be seen from Route H, if you watch for traffic. A sign at the cemetery gates makes that clear for the cemetery too. It is only open from dawn till dusk. I'm not sure I would want to be there after dusk anyway; the cross is spooky. The light was supposed to appear in 2002. The next time it should show up is in 2009. But whether it shows up or not, the locals think Bone Hill is special.

"Whether it's the ghost or it's gas," Vicki said, "there's something going on out there."

Bone Hill

Driving directions: From Levasy, take Route H south for one and a half miles, then turn right on West Bonehill Road.

Hours: daylight to dusk.

Chapter 4

Fort Osage
SIBLEY

A few flakes of snow blew in the frosty wind buffeting Fort Osage. A lot of things had hit the original wooden structure after it was erected in 1808 under the direction of William Clark (of the Lewis and Clark expedition). But most of today's Fort Osage, built in the 1940s, is a replica of the old fort. The wind was not the worst of this fort's problems. The compound, its fortifications originally made of local trees carved into spikes by workers with rough metal axes, overlooks the muddy Missouri River, just as it did when it was an outpost of the brand new Louisiana Purchase. The young fort housed soldiers who guarded the new territory and a trading post called the United States Factory Trade House, as well as providing protection for people traveling west.

As I walked into the fort, passing under the dark, looming structure of Bunkhouse No. 4, the February wind bit through my jacket. I wondered how the soldiers of two hundred years ago might have handled the cold without the benefit of twenty-first century outdoor gear from L.L.Bean. As I stopped at a deserted campfire to try and warm up, I realized those soldiers probably didn't care how cold it was when someone was shooting a musket at them.

Throughout its functional history, Fort Osage was a safe haven for those who were cold, hungry, and lost. Now, the old fort may be a haven for people who have never left. I walked through the compound, the sterile emptiness of winter rendering this Jackson County tourist attraction quiet—too quiet. I worked my way to the building where the historic interpreters dressed, and entered a haven of natural gas-supplied warmth. Site administrator Steve Wilson greeted me in full 1808 soldier gear. Cool. Steve has experienced a lot of things during his years at the fort, but there are a few of them he cannot explain.

"I started working here in March 1993," Steve said looking at me from behind his tiny, round period lenses mounted in gold metal frames. "The very first experience I had was within two weeks after I started. We had to lock up one Sunday and I made the mistake of whistling, which was taboo to the Osage Indians." Because the Osage controlled a great swath of Missouri, it was important to make friends with them as the young United States government made its way into the Midwest. George Champlain Sibley, an agent for U.S. Factory Trade, and his wife, Mary, moved to the area to run the factory at Fort Osage in 1816. In between hosting celebrities like Daniel Boone and naturalist John James Audubon, they made friends with the Osage Indians, but there were still a few cultural problems.

"You don't point with your finger and you don't whistle," Steve said. "If [I] point at someone, that means I'll do something violent to you. If you whistled, you invited the Woluska. They're tiny, little people," he continued, holding his right hand a few inches above his left. "They're equivalent to European trolls. When you whistled, they jumped in your mouth to punish you. If they went up, you got severe headaches. If they went down, you got severe stomachaches."

But in 1993, Steve did not think twice about whistling—until he did it. "As I began to whistle, you know how you get the heebie-jeebies?" he said. "My hair stood up and I could feel this pressure on my chest and on my back.

And I shut the shutters and exited the factory and it stopped immediately. It made my hair stand on end. It was like you were around static electricity."

For the record, Steve did not actually see the Woluska, but the experience was still something he couldn't explain. Neither were the footsteps. In January or February 1994, Steve and historical site interpreter Phil Schulze were the only people at the fort when Steve received a visitor in the factory. "I heard steps on the stairs above me from the north wall to Sibley's bedroom," he said. "You could hear every step. Heel, toe. Heel, toe. Every time the toe hit there was a metallic ring. The door was shut. I don't know how anyone could get into or out of the building." So he went upstairs to investigate. "No one was there. I thought that was very bizarre."

Soon after, Steve's new boots arrived. He lifted his right leg and dropped his boot-shod foot on the commons table to show it to me, rattling a couple of coffee cups in the process. His boots were heavy black leather period military issue with metal studs across the toe and a metal plate on the heel. Probably good for traction, but I got tired just thinking about wearing them. "Some months after I'd heard the sound, I was in the factory walking around," Steve said. "And I realized where the sound came from. A loose heel plate." But Steve was the only person at the fort with that style of boot. Well, the only live person.

Steve may have seen the man who wore those boots a year later, in 1995. "We had a volunteer here, a history professor, when we were sitting in [the factory], I saw a man walk by the window," Steve said. "He's dressed in black. He's got a period-correct vest, round hat, a ruffled shirt. I know all the volunteers and didn't recognize him. I ran outside and he wasn't there." Stepping onto the wooden walkway that surrounds the factory with his metal-shod boots, Steve went looking for the man, but didn't find him. But someone at the fort had seen the black-clad man before.

"Nobody around was dressed like that," Steve said. "The description of the guy was the same as the description from a family from out of state. They'd asked if they could get a picture with him. He acquiesced. When the picture was developed, there was the family, but there was a gap where the guy was." But it was not just the matching description of the man that piqued Steve's interest—it was the noise of the man's boots. "When the guy walked by, I could hear the same metallic clink."

Did Steve see a ghost? It's possible. Other people at Fort Osage have. In 2004, a reenactor sleeping in the factory during a militia muster saw the stone

hearth radiating a rainbow of colors at 4:00 AM while others in the factory heard people running up and down the stairs. But at the militia muster in 1995, a ghost sighting became personal for Steve Wilson. "One of our volunteers and I volunteered to sleep in Sibley's bedroom," Steve said. "At some point in the night, Blake woke up because someone had walked into the room." According to Steve, the doors of the building were locked from the inside and could only be opened from the inside. The visitor appeared to be a traditionally dressed Osage Indian. "[Blake] said, 'I thought it was Dave,' who portrayed an Osage Indian. 'He bent over you and started talking in your ear.'" Steve didn't wake up during the encounter, but what happened is something that still puzzles him. "[The ghost] was speaking in Osage, and when we translated it, apparently what he was asking was, 'Are you warm enough?'"

If the figure in the night was the spirit of an Osage Indian, it wouldn't be the first time a member of the Osage tribe got into the fort after dark. "We do have historic precedent of Indians sneaking into Sibley's bedroom," Steve told me. During a time when the Osage and the Iowa Indians were at war, a group of Osage killed an Iowa scout and beheaded him. To show his prowess, the Osage Indian Sans Oreille (called "Man without Ears" because he wouldn't listen to anyone's advice) snuck into Sibley's bedroom and, by torchlight, showed Sibley the Iowa Indian's severed head, Steve said, "to show how good they did their job." Was this apparition the same Sans Oreille who would have probably earned a pretty good parking spot in today's corporate world for a job well done? Maybe. According to an Osage Indian delegation that visited Fort Osage in the mid-1990s, the ghosts at the fort are pretty easygoing. "One [delegate] was a tribal elder," said Steve. "As he walked around the grounds, to just get a sense of the feeling, he told me what he could sense off the spirits, and they were peaceful."

Stepping outside the log building, I walked along the wooden walkway around the factory. The rubber soles of my machine-made leather shoes made no sound in the cold morning; a metal-shod boot would have rung across the grounds. I was sure Steve had not imagined anything. "I was brought up not to believe in this stuff," he said. "My mom and dad [would say] that's all malarkey. But with these things around here, it kind of challenged my thinking."

Phil Schulze has worked as a historical site interpreter at the fort since 1990 and has experienced strange things he can't explain either, but they do not bother him. "I don't think our ghosts are malicious," he said. Phil, who portrays a pre-1812 soldier, has seen and heard things he can't explain. "Many, many years ago one cold winter's morning, I was down here [at the factory] by myself," he began. "It was very quiet." Snow started to fall as Phil made his way down to the factory that morning and it continued to build up as he waited for visitors. Then he got one he didn't expect.

"I was sitting inside the dining room," Phil continued. "All of a sudden I heard footsteps out on the porch going toward the door. I got up and opened the front door and saw nothing." Phil was certain he had heard someone walking along the wooden walkway toward the factory. He was not completely surprised to find nobody there, but he wasn't prepared for what he did see. "What really startled me," he said, "[was that] there were

footprints in the light cover of snow leading up to the door. I have no explanation for that, but it raised the hair on the back of my neck." He had
the same reaction when he heard people working in the factory storeroom.
"One morning, I was down here by myself," Phil said. "I heard these noises
upstairs. It startled me so much I left the building. I didn't really want to go
upstairs. I collected myself and I went back, and didn't see anything."

Back in the 1990s, a woman worked as a cook for the fort, cooking as
they did in the early 1800s over a great fire in the hearth in the basement of
the factory. The metal hooks where cooks hung their pots still swing over
the fire there, and the cook was bending over one of those pots when, Phil
reported, she had a visitor. "[She] wasn't a big believer in ghosts. But one
morning she was cooking over the open hearth here. She was bent over
and then she heard a wooden spoon behind her on the floor." Phil pulled
a heavy wooden spoon from a crock full of spoons about eight feet away
from the hearth and tossed it onto the floor near the hearth. "She turned
and saw the spoon," he said. "For some reason it flew out of the crock eight
feet and startled her. She had no explanation for it. Maybe a cook who was
here two hundred years ago was pulling a prank on her." Phil added, "A lot
of this I'm sure has logical explanations. But some of it makes you wonder.
It's a little scary, but I'm not really afraid of it."

Although the factory seems to be the center of spirit activity, it is not
the only place at Fort Osage people have experienced otherworldly things.
"We've had a few visitors who have weird feelings by Bunkhouse No. 4,"
Phil said. "There's an old story of the ghostly soldier. There's been people
through the years who've seen him in full dress uniform, musket, and ac-
coutrements, as if he's standing on guard duty. But he disappears if someone gets near." I wanted to see that for myself. I made my way across the
compound to the square wooden structure of Bunkhouse No. 4, its open
door allowing in little of the midday sun. The bunkhouse, with a watchtower on the second floor, was small. A staircase, almost black in the dim
light, leads upstairs where two-hundred-year-old dead soldiers once held
watch. I readied my camera and climbed the dark stairs. Upstairs in the
tower, slits for the barrels of muskets allowed in the only light, giving the
room an equal cast of gray. Any ghosts of dead soldiers? Not today. But the
air in the watchtower was stuffy, warm, and claustrophobic—and I don't
usually get claustrophobic. I snapped a couple of shots, hoping to capture
an orb, or at least some good graffiti, and left.

"People have felt it's an unfriendly place to be at," Phil said. "They get a bad feeling walking past." They're right—Bunkhouse No. 4 is kind of creepy. I left the fort, passing the campfire that had burned down to embers, Looking back at the place William Clark thought would be a good spot to camp, I wondered how many souls had passed through this outpost and how many stayed…especially at the factory.

Old buildings make noises, bt Steve said people hear noises that even an old building cannot make. "The footsteps? How do I understand that? Somebody made that noise. The boots? I can't account for that. I just chalk it up to things that happen and I don't worry about it." Steve took the attitude that "weird things happen. Maybe they happen for a reason. I don't know. They just happen."

Fort Osage Historic Site

105 Osage Street, Sibley, MO 64088

Phone: 816/650-5737
Website: www.historicfortosage.com
Hours: March 1 through November 15: 9 AM–4:30 PM; Tuesday through Sunday; November 16 through February 28: 9 AM–4:30 PM Saturday and Sunday
Admission: adults $5; youth and seniors $3; under 5 free

Chapter 5

Lone Jack Battlefield
LONE JACK

The small, round building is hard to see from the street. I pulled into the concrete parking lot east of Lone Jack's Bynum Road after noticing a roadside historical marker visible only because I had been looking for it. The sign read "Battle of Lone Jack." This was once a state park in a rural area, but the same encroaching development that turned the area into a suburb of Kansas City has rendered the historic spot almost forgotten except by Civil War buffs, Rooster Cogburn, and a local historical society. But the people who love Lone Jack know it's there, and they are proud of their town and its past. "This town has a 175-year-old history," said John Drago, former director of the museum. "People were settling here the year Beethoven died. That tells you how old this town is."

The historic site sits a few blocks off US 50, the paths of American Indians, settlers, and Civil War soldiers now severed by asphalt and tractor-trailers traveling between Kansas City and St. Louis. I had pulled off that highway to get to the museum and, as I got out of my car, I noticed a piece of history untouched by modern times or asphalt—1800s hedgerows were still visible around an old cemetery behind the museum. Lone Jack, with a population of about 600, is peaceful, as small midwestern towns tend to be. There is a video rental store and a café on the highway, churches have chili dinners, and in the fall, people turn out to watch their 1-A school's team, the Mules, play football.

But in 1862, this quiet town paid a one-day visit to hell. "It was the bloodiest fight in the Civil War in Missouri," John reported. "Four to five thousand men fought and the town was almost destroyed. You can't hardly throw a rock around here without hitting a cemetery." Sometimes, the battle between the North and the South rages on. Reports of Civil War soldiers still roaming the battlefield are not uncommon. "I know there's things here," John said. "I hear about them all the time."

John greeted me inside the round museum building, where racks of pamphlets and bins of bonnets and Civil War-replica military caps decorated the front hall. The room was cold, but then again, it was February. "You're sitting in the middle of what was called New Town," John said. "In 1828, there was already a settlement here." White settlers built Lone Jack on the Shawnee Trace, an American Indian thoroughfare. "This was a rise on the ground where the Indians would come out of the winter grounds and prepare for their spring hunt," John told me. "And the only landmark on this rise was a giant Jack Oak tree." By the time of the Civil War, Lone Jack had five major crossroads coming through town. "If you went north, south, east, or west, Lone Jack was the way you came through," John said. "By 1861, it was literally the crossroads to come through Missouri."

On August 15, 1862, the population of the town was more than 1,500. By the end of the following day, the population would be much less. "August 16, 1862, was the Battle of Lone Jack," John said. "There were five independent Confederate camps within the area of Lone Jack." Union forces entering the area attacked, and the battle quickly turned into an urban house-to-house fight between 800 Union and 2,400 Confederate troops. The Union troops shot cannons into every house to dislodge Confederates. Figures like William Quantrill, Upton Hayes, and Cole Younger were involved in the battle. The Confederates eventually won the battle, but only after numerous charges, retreats, and counterattacks, during which a battery of cannons changed hands five times.

"The battle was a real cluster mess," John continued. "There were 115 dead horses just in the town square. One hundred forty-plus soldiers just in the town square. It was August, 100-degree heat. Men were buried in trenches. It took weeks to clean the horses out of town. A soldier coming in next day wrote there wasn't a place on the ground that wasn't beat up by the battle. It took a long time to get it cleaned up." More than 10,000 Civil War artifacts have been excavated from a field across the street from the museum, including uniform buttons, coins, gun pieces, lead shot, and cannon balls. The government respects the history of the site. "We're not allowed to plant a flower here without an archeologist present," John said.

But some less physical memories of the Civil War remain here. Steve Garrett grew up in Lone Jack and, though he is now a Civil War reenactor who makes his living bartending in nearby Grain Valley, his experience with the Battle of Lone Jack happened long before adulthood. One night in the late 1970s, when Steve was thirteen or fourteen years old, he and his friend Mark were riding dirt bikes, looking for a party in a field. Now that empty field is a housing development; in August 1862 it was a battlefield. "As we were going past the museum we saw a campfire and we figured they were out there," he said. "The fire was pretty much across from the cemetery. It was behind it. We heard a campfire crackling, and you could see the smoke in the air, everything. You could see it burn through the hedgerow. We only had our back to it twenty seconds as we were going through the [cemetery] fence."

They didn't expect what they found. "The field was freshly plowed and the fire was gone," Steve said. "Mark turned to me and said, 'Did you feel that?' It felt like ice water run down my back. There was no sign of anything. There wasn't the smell of smoke anymore. It was gone." By the time Steve and Mark ran back to their bikes, the fire had reappeared. "That fire was burning bright as day," Steve said. "There's no way there was a fire there. It was way weird. I've seen a fire out there burning one or two times since then."

Steve's encounter is common. "People at night see what appears to be a campfire," John said. "But when they investigated, they didn't find anything. It was dark or foggy and there were fires in the field, but you couldn't get close to them. This was common from the people from the mid-1800s to the

1990s. There was a battle in that field. There was a lot of heavy fighting."

A psychic visiting the battlefield confirmed Steve's encounter. "There was a psychic lady out there and as far as I know, we never really told anybody about it, she was explaining about a campsite right over here at the edge of the cemetery," Steve said. "This lady was telling me, 'Well, what do *you* know about a campfire?' I said, 'You tell me what you're seeing and I'll tell you what I know.' She was real close, within ten feet. She just nailed things." The same psychic also found a previously unknown trench of buried soldiers. People at the museum are keeping an open mind about psychics and the spirits at the Lone Jack battlefield because the strange occurrences still make them curious.

"I'm a Missourian, so I'm as skeptical as it gets about anything," Steve said. "But being a reenactor I've seen a few things that made me check my skepticism at the door." Early in Steve's career as a Civil War reenactor, he saw something more than a phantom fire at the historic site. "When we're in camp, it's run like a military unit," he said. "You've got duties. We have a fire watch. We rotate in the night

to keep an eye on the fire and on the surroundings." Which included watching the horses. "I was on fire watch," he said. "It was about two o'clock in the morning or so. I was supposed to wake up my relief. I was sitting there and another guy was up with me. In the field next to the road where we were going to do our re-enactment battle, I saw a guy out there riding his horse. He'd ride a few paces and lean over like he was messing with the saddle." Steve woke his relief to find out who the late-night rider was. "We figured it was Dan out there riding. The way the hat looked and the horse looked like Dan. Sure enough, Dan's tent was empty."

But Dan was out of camp that night and he did not come back until the next day. "I asked anyone in camp and there was nobody out riding," Steve said. "There was a horse and a rider out in that field and they ran over that north ridge near the highway." It wasn't until Steve drove his truck to the store that he saw it could not have been Dan or anyone else running over the north ridge. "He was riding down the hill," he contiued. "But there's not a hill there anymore. They cut it out for the highway. It's a cliff. To this day I don't know. There was somebody out there."

Alinda M. Miller, president of The Friends of Historic Lone Jack, Inc., said the sightings have been prevalent for a long time. "We haven't had any of our volunteers reporting ghosts; however, our townsfolk have reported seeing them," she said. "We've had reports that an old farmer, about sixty years ago, he'd see them when he'd be out plowing—soldiers." I didn't see any soldiers in the cemetery, but, then again, it was about twenty-five degrees outside. If I were a soldier, I wouldn't have been around if I had not been ordered to. Walking from the Lone Jack Battlefield Museum to the cemetery, I touched the trees planted in rows by people of another age, and I traced my index finger around an empty hole once home to a gold, five-pointed star set in the Civil War monument vandalized decades ago by people still feeling the sting of the war. The Civil War pain wasn't there for me.

For Steve's former girlfriend, it was enough that somebody paid her a visit. Steve has done maintenance at the museum as a volunteer and one night in 2004, he and his girlfriend were alone at the museum. "She did not like being there at all," Steve said. "I left something out in the truck and I'd told her to go out and get it for me. Shortly I heard the door open and the door close again. She came around the corner and she was bone pale." She had seen something that made her want to never return. "When she came in her mouth was moving and no words were coming out," Steve said. "I was kind of freaked out at first. I finally got her sat down and she said, 'We have to leave now.'" She had seen men standing in the cemetery. "She said, 'There were these three guys and they had rifles and they walked into the trees,'" Steve reported.

He had heard this story before. "There was an old man who was a like a second grandfather to me when I was a kid who told us ghost stories," he said. "What she described was the Three Wise Men just as the old man told me. There were three guys who were on guard at the cemetery. They'd walk back and forth and they'd all just disappear. Somebody who wasn't from around here saw the same thing the old man described. I wished I'd seen it."

Yeah, me, too. Walking down the long sidewalk from the Civil War cemetery to the parking lot, I thought of the history of this small town, a town that was almost torn apart in a war from which I'm generations removed. I am just happy I wasn't there in 1862. "The hatred's been in this community for a very long time," John said. "The town still survived. There's a tenacity of the community. This is a community driven to survive." Even after death.

Lone Jack Battlefield Museum

301 South Bynum Road, Lone Jack, MO 64070

Phone: 816/697-8833
E-mail: lonejackmuseum@kc.rr.com
Website: www.historiclonejack.org/museum
Hours: April through October: 10 AM–4 PM Wednesday through Saturday, 1 PM–4 PM Sunday; November through March: 10 AM–4 PM Saturday, 1 PM–4 PM Sunday
Admission: adults $3; children (12 and under) $1; seniors $2

Wilson's Creek National Battlefield

REPUBLIC

Thick, waist-high native prairie grass covers the valley floor at Wilson's Creek National Battlefield. The valley, surrounded by a heavy ring of trees, seemed to move slightly as a warm summer breeze sifted through the grass and tall weeds. A deer drinking from Wilson's Creek ignored me as I drove over a concrete bridge on my way through the 1,750-acre battlefield. Living in a national park does have some benefits for wildlife—nobody shoots at them. I stopped at the parking lot of the John Ray House on the first leg of my journey and turned off the car. A wild turkey gobbled somewhere to my left as I stepped out of the car and looked into the afternoon. I was alone on the small hill that overlooked part of the valley where the first major Western battle of the Civil War raged for six hours in 1861. A lone

red-tailed hawk was suspended motionless in an updraft above me. If it weren't for the insects buzzing in the grass and the tom trying to flirt with a hen somewhere in the brush, I would have thought I was in one of those apocalyptic "last person left alive" science fiction movies, but without all the zombies.

The Battle of Wilson's Creek began the morning of August 10, 1861. General Nathaniel Lyon of the Union Army set out a few months before to secure Missouri for the Union. From St. Louis, Lyon made his way through various skirmishes to this spot ten miles south of Springfield where his army of 5,400 met an army of about 12,000 Confederate soldiers. More than 2,500 soldiers were killed, wounded, or captured during that battle. The Confederate forces lost 12 percent of its troops; the Union army lost 24 percent of its troops, including General Lyon. Without their general and low on ammunition, the Union army retreated to Springfield.

One hundred years later, the battlefield was dedicated as a national park. Looking across the valley from the John Ray House, I could almost see Bloody Hill, the site of the main battle. John Ray and his family probably witnessed the battle through the few trees that dotted the valley floor. I probably wouldn't get to Bloody Hill for at least an hour. First I wanted to visit a spot in the grass where part of the battle raged, with Confederate soldiers shooting at their Union brothers. But I was not there to relive their fight, I was there trying to catch a glimpse of a 145-year-old resident of Wilson's Creek.

John Ray was a farmer and the postmaster of Wilson's Creek. His house, built in 1850, was the Wilson Creek Post Office for ten years and housed himself, his wife, Roxanna, their nine children, and a mail carrier. From the parking lot, I couldn't see the house. It was farther up the hill, obscured by tall grass that gave a bit of a "Little House on the Prairie" feel to the place. But I could see the Ray springhouse, a small stone building in the valley that covered a spring where the Ray children fetched water and stored perishables like milk, eggs, and butter. The Ray children also brought water up from that small building when Confederate soldiers occupied their house during the battle.

Although the Rays died long ago, at least one member of the Ray family may still be at Wilson's Creek. Ranger Dana Maanum said visitors have reported seeing someone walking up the hill through the tall grass to the Ray house—someone who should not be there. "There was a young woman in period clothing carrying well water through the grass," Dana said. "The people who saw it thought it was a girl in a living history program. They called out to her and she didn't respond. We didn't have a living history program at that time." One of Ray's daughters, perhaps?

As I stood in front of the Ray house, looking across the field that stretched to the bottom of the valley, I noticed a swath cut in the knee-high grass. Weeds were pushed down as if someone had been walking through that grass to get to the springhouse. Of course, a deer could have made that path, or maybe a visitor who wanted to take a Julie Andrews *Sound of Music* spin down the hill. Then again, it could have been one of the Ray children going down to the well. Did a ghost live at the Ray house? "With all the deaths out here," Maanum said, "it might be." Ranger Connie Langum does not believe in the battlefield ghosts. "I've been here twelve years and I've not heard one," she said. "I've not seen one." Chief Ranger John Sutton does not believe in the ghosts either. "I've been here sixteen years," he told me. "I've been here all times of day and night and I have never experienced anything out of normal. You always run into people who say they experience things out of normal. People have heard odd sounds they've interpreted as moans or tramping soldiers. We had this one group come out here a number of years ago, about ten years ago, wanting to do some photography or something. A ranger stayed out here with them and nothing happened. I don't put much credit in ghost stories."

But some people do. Area resident Lee Prosser has seen and heard enough otherworldly activity at Wilson's Creek to convince him there's something ghostly there. And why not? It runs in his family. Lee's father, Harold Prosser, and his uncles Billy Bob and Willard Firestone, were fishing near the battlefield before World War II when they saw something they didn't expect. "According to my uncle's notes, it was early August in 1940. They fished near the Wilson's Creek Battlefield. It was early dusk. They saw five men and they were dressed in Union army clothes. They walked past them. They were carrying rifles and were plainly visible. They were fifteen feet from the fishermen and the soldiers just faded away."

But that wasn't the last time Lee's family would see the soldiers. "When I was with my uncle Willard, it was probably in August of 1953, I wasn't even a teenager," Lee said. "We saw these same guys carrying the rifles. It was the same area. They were just walking, and as soon as they were there they were gone. They're so vivid they're still there. They're intact. There's a

loop in time there that makes that possible." The sightings reach far back
into Lee's memory. "As far back as I can recall, it just seemed like you'd see
a squad of troops on bivouac," he explained. "They walk by you and that's
that. It was like they had a purpose and they knew where they were going
and they were gone. Of all the sites, over the last maybe one hundred years,
Wilson's Battlefield Creek, that area is full of ghost stories. There are things
going on there today."

If there is anyplace worthy of a haunting at the Wilson's Creek battlefield, it should be Bloody Hill, the site of one of the most deadly fights of
the Civil War. Union artillery batteries on Bloody Hill dueled with Confederate batteries in the valley and across the creek for six hours. The Union
soldiers were outnumbered two to one, and losses were heavy. General
Lyon was killed, and by 11:00 AM the Union army's ammunition was nearly
gone. Five cannons still sit on Bloody Hill staring down a few cannons
that dot the bottom of the valley. The ones atop the hill were made in the
mid-nineteenth century at the N. P. Ames Foundry in Springfield, Mas-
sachusetts. I walked around those cannons, feeling the hot metal, but the
heat came from the sun, not weapons' fire. I thought if there were anyplace
on the battlefield I might feel something paranormal, it should be the spot
where soldiers were massacred by the hundreds. But the only thing I heard

was an occasional car passing by on Route ZZ.

Civil War buff Troy Chrisman of Blue Springs has visited Wilson's Creek Battlefield many times, but a few years ago he felt something he had not experienced before. "I'd been on the Bloody Hill before. It seems like every time I go it's always kind of cool," Troy said. "It was creeping up on dusk, then I noticed I'm the only one up there. It was kind of creepy on a battlefield anyway. It kind of hit me. I kind of don't need to be here. I remember looking behind me. You feel like you want to look around and see where you are, catch your bearings. I just wanted to get off the hill. On a Civil War battlefield, you get this feeling that you're not alone here, and I know this is where I don't need to be right now. It wasn't that it was scary, but I didn't need to be up on that hill."

Standing on Bloody Hill, I noticed that, yeah, it was quiet. Too quiet for an afternoon. Too quiet for a site that had a parking lot teeming with cars. And too quiet to be up there alone with your imagination. I was alone, but it didn't feel like it. I snapped a few shots and left, sliding into my car and driving the long, winding path to the exit. Wilson's Creek National Battlefield is peaceful, beautiful, and well-kept. And on a particularly quiet day, if you listen closely enough, you might hear the swish of prairie grass against the leather boots of soldiers marching away as their comrades lay dying. No, really. You might.

Wilson's Creek National Battlefield

6424 West Farm Road 182, Republic, MO 65738

Phone: 417/732-2662, ext. 227
Website: www.nps.gov/wicr
Hours: March through October, 8 AM–5 PM; November through February: 8 AM–5 PM Wednesday through Sunday
Admission: adults $5; maximum of $10 per vehicle

Chapter 7

Kendrick House
CARTHAGE

Iron rods run the length of the Kendrick House. In the late nineteenth century, a salesman came through Carthage hawking a system of iron rods designed to keep the walls of the buyer's house from bowing and spreading apart. The rods bolt on the outside of the building and run through the interior of the house—not inside the walls and out of the way, but out in the open, creating something that fits in the gray space between practical and downright weird. The man sold quite a few of these systems throughout Carthage and probably never came back to town.

I pulled into the gravel drive of the house, and parked next to a six-foot model of the two-story home that sat alone in the yard. I wondered if the model was used for a play, a promotion, or perhaps as a home for elves. The Kendrick House is north of Carthage, not as far out of town as it was 151 years ago when the slaves of Sinnet and Elizabeth Rankin built the three-brick thick, four-room house on 17,000 acres, but still far enough that encroaching stoplights

of the city have not yet reached it. "It was a long, long way out of town at that time," said my guide, Roberta Williams, a member of the board of directors of Kendrick House. "I think that's why the soldiers occupied it."

Carthage was the site of two battles during the Civil War: one in 1861, the other in 1864. A strategic location for an army, the house had been completed in 1854, but William Kendrick didn't buy it until 1860. Shortly after moving in, the Kendricks decided to abandon their new home and travel to nearby Neosho in Newton County, when the Southern guerrillas set fire to Carthage in 1864. "During the war, the Kendrick family fled. They watched the town being burned," according to Roberta. "They were on the balcony, and they were actually watching the town being burned. They said they could see buggies and people being burned in the sky."

Because of its size and distance from town, the house was used at various times by Union and Confederate forces. It was a general headquarters, a hospital, and a hideout. "Soldiers brought the horses in so they wouldn't be stolen and so the [other side] wouldn't know they were in the house," Roberta said.

"When the Kendricks came back after the war, they found hoof prints in the wood. The house was new so the wood was still soft."

I knelt and ran my finger around the U-shape of a horseshoe print in the floor of the sitting room. The horse that made that mark was probably in battle during the most violent time in our nation's history. I was not sure if that print was important, but it was kinda neat. To complete the Civil

War trappings, a door on the floor led to a tunnel for the Underground Railroad, Roberta told me, although after 150 years, the five-mile-long tunnel has caved in. The house has been lived in, more or less continuously, since it was built. A back part of the house, with a kitchen and a bathroom, has been "torn down, put together, torn down, put together since '54," Roberta continued, until a group called Victorian Carthage bought it in 1989 and turned it into a historic attraction and meeting place. But the group also bought the home's tumultuous history. "A lot of people died here," said Roberta. "This was once used as a birthing house and a lot of them didn't make it. There were slaves murdered on the property. There was a lady they hung from a tree out back."

The home's tumultuous history has left its own imprint on Kendrick House—an otherworldly imprint. Roberta sometimes opens up the house for tours, and has gone there in the early morning hours to prepare for a large group breakfast, one of the ways the board of directors pays for the upkeep on the house. "There's times when I've heard people whisper," she said. "It's kind of scary. I just don't try and think about it when I'm out here by myself." Sometimes, though, she can't help but think about it. "Some of the incidents have occurred when I come out here—I'll set up a glass [upside down on the table in preparation for a dinner], and later a glass will be turned upright. The other day it happened to me. I knew I had the glass upside down and when I came back in the room, it was right side up. I was the only one here."

I didn't notice anything odd as we walked through the Kendrick House, apart from those iron rods running along the sides of the rooms and the fact that at some point in the home's history, someone had painted the stairs mauve. Upstairs, Roberta showed me the bedrooms, one of which contained a cradle originally owned by the Kendrick family. Although the cradle has never been involved in anything other than being a cradle, something in the house does not like the way the beds are made or the way period clothes are arranged on them. "You can go out there and make sure the bed's all fluffed out and go in not an hour later, and the bed is pushed in again and the children's clothes are on the floor," Roberta said. "You're the only one out there. A lot of times I quit putting the clothes on the bed because whoever or whatever doesn't like the clothes on the bed."

Although Roberta has also heard footsteps in the house when she was alone, has had to close curtains she had closed just minutes before, and has seen a "golden glow" glide back and forth across the Kendrick House's kitchen window, she is certain other people have experienced something ghostly at the Kendrick House too. "Missouri Southern [State University –Joplin] came out there twice and they've stayed all night and they've seen images out here," she explained. "And the trucking company [next door], and I say they're drunk, but a driver came in one night and saw children playing in the backyard with a ball. I'm not saying they don't exist. But you feel like there's people watching you and sometimes they could be. My husband tells me the house gives him the creeps. He wouldn't live here."

Kendrick House

131 Northwoods Route V at Garrison, Carthage, MO 64836

Phone: 417/358-0636
E-mail: Director@KendrickPlace.com
Website: www.kendrickplace.com
Tours: 10 AM–4 PM, Tuesday through Saturday, or by appointment.

This is My House

Some people are proud of their homes, especially if they are the first own-ers. Mansions built by lumber barons, beer barons, postmasters, and railroad tycoons dot this state. The mansions were never meant to sit silently; today many are open to parties and public tours. But these homes hold more than high-ceilinged halls, mahogany staircases, and marble fireplaces. The homes, right down to their foundations, embrace the company of their former own-ers who remain to watch over their earthly pride and joy—maybe forever.

Chapter 8

Rockcliffe Mansion
HANNIBAL

John Cruikshank comes home some nights at 2:00 AM. He sneaks in the creaky door of a servant's entrance, walks up the back staircase, and goes down the hall to his second-floor bedroom at Rockcliffe Mansion—but he doesn't do this every night. "We'd been here for two years before we heard Mr. Cruikshank come in," said Mary McAvoy, who lived as caretaker of the building with her husband, Jerry, for twelve years until June 2005. "It woke me up." It probably would not have bothered her if John Cruikshank hadn't been dead since 1924.

Saturday morning may not the best time to look for ghosts, but spirits are not predictable. A three and a half-story, thirty-room turn of the century mansion sits atop a rocky hill overlooking downtown Hannibal and a stretch of the Mississippi River that a young Mark Twain fell in love with. As I walked down the winding driveway to the mansion's entrance

on Bird Street, the morning sun on the great, gray-brick home, with its Grecian columns and clay-tiled roof, threw a shadow large enough to hide another house. When Rockcliffe Mansion was built in 1900, it was outside town, but now it is almost downtown. The house cannot be seen from the street, where crumbling stone stairs used now only by tourists led me up the hill. As I left street level, the mansion, with its ten front-facing windows, loomed suddenly into view. The sight was impressive now. I could only image how it looked to guests and curious passersby when it was new. Now, over a century later, the mansion is supposedly haunted. Was something watching my long approach from an upstairs window? Was the spirit of some long-dead Missouri aristocrat staring at me through the antique curtains? Was the restless soul of some....

No. Nobody was there. I looked.

Crying stone cherubs, their once sharp features softened by weather, greeted me as I explored the grounds around the mansion's front entrance. The statues were probably beautiful in 1900. Now, with dark weathered lines beneath their eyes, they were a bit creepy. I walked to the front door and opened it. No need to knock. Rockcliffe Mansion is on the National Register of Historic places. It's open for tours—including a monthly ghost tour of Hannibal. The house has reportedly only shifted on its foundation one-sixteenth of an inch since it was built. The double-brick construction has served it well over the past century, as have the imported oak, walnut, and mahogany that adorn the interior. An abundance of wood doors, trim, and paneling on the ground floor of the mansion keep it dark. A nice mood setter.

Mary McAvoy greeted me from behind a desk and invited me to sit in a high-backed, century-old chair that would have looked natural in a museum, or maybe Camelot. There was a tour going through, she said, so we might be interrupted. We were—several times. But Mary, with stark white hair and a bright smile, never lost her place or patience as she told me about the ghosts of Rockcliffe Mansion. Mary met John Cruikshank in 1995 while she was caretaker of the mansion. Her husband had gone to a class reunion in Bloomington, Illinois, and Mary thought it might be unnerving to sleep in their third-floor apartment alone—so she moved to the second-floor guest room next to the servant stairs. Maybe she should have stayed in her room. "I woke up at two in the morning with the side door banging, and I thought it was my husband," Mary said. "And I told him not to go to the third floor—but the footsteps just kept coming. I said, 'This isn't funny.'" Then Mary looked into the hallway where she heard the footsteps. "But there was no one there."

John visited the McAvoys more after that—in their apartment. "About a quarter of nine the room filled up with heavy, heavy cigar smoke," Mary said. "You didn't see it, but there was a heavy, heavy smell. But no one smokes in the house. You're not allowed." Except John. He had earned it. It took Cruikshank two years to build Rockcliffe Mansion. The 5 feet 4 inch tall lumber baron envisioned a magnificent home atop a rocky cliff overlooking Hannibal and the Mississippi River. "He wanted to have the biggest house and the grandest house in the state of Missouri," Mary said. "And he did." Cruikshank moved his wife and four daughters into what the *St. Louis Post-Dispatch* then called "the finest home in Missouri." Mark Twain even gave his "good-bye to Hannibal" speech from the mansion's grand staircase to three hundred people in 1902. After John Cruikshank's death, his wife moved out of Rockcliffe, abandoning it to the spiders and vandals. Although the mansion sat abandoned for forty-three years, it hardly sat empty. There remains the original woodwork—all restored—much of the glass, imported hand-carved furnishings, original 1900 state-of-the-art electric lights, thermostats, and, oh, yes … the ghosts.

"The house is haunted," Mary said. "Mr. Cruikshank is here. And his wife is here. And one daughter is here." Mary is not the only one to experience them. "We've had four or five different people who've had a sighting. Three tour guides. Different people at different times."

I went into the ground floor kitchen where people have seen John standing by the bar. No one was in the kitchen, which was good for me. People don't usually see a ghost when others are around to verify it. There were no cold spots in the kitchen, no chills, no unexplained smells, and no blood running down the walls. John must not have been hungry the day I visited. But he has visited some. "They go into the room and he's standing there and he just dissolves," Mary said. "A short man. He has white hair, goatee, and mustache. He's always wearing a brown felt hat and a suit. A period suit. He's standing there, only for a second or two. And then he dissolves." Portraits of John Cruikshank and his wife hang above a bookshelf holding late-nineteenth and early-twentieth century reference books in the first floor receiving room, so visitors to the mansion may already know what the former owner looks like before they have a "sighting." But then again.…

During a regular ghost tour of Hannibal, Rockcliffe owner Rick Rose took a tour of sixty people through the ground floor of the mansion. I paid my $15 to join the tour and see what mysteries Hannibal had to offer. Crowded in the receiving room, some of the dowsing rods Rick provided twisted in their hands to signify an unseen disturbance. A handheld sensor designed to detect electromagnetic fields associated with spirits registered something strange around John Cruikshank's picture, but not Mrs. Cruikshank's picture just inches away. "Would you look at that," said one of the sixty guests packed into the room. Most looked her way. Rick said he had seen the sensor go off near John Cruikshank's picture before, so he has tried to find an electrical explanation in the wall—there isn't one. "We looked and there was just an old inactive fuse box," Rick explained, emphasizing that the box is not hooked to live electricity. "And [the reading] is not at her picture—it's just his."

Maybe Mr. Cruikshank just had too much of his personality invested in the house to give up ownership quietly. Candace Klemann, a Hannibal transplant from California, is sensitive to the other side. "What I sense in that house is he was kind of a bastard," Candace said. "He wasn't a very nice person. The fact that [his wife] left as soon as he died tells you something."

Candace helped lead one of the two ghost tours that day. There was not any activity on her tour. But Mary said with normal mansion tours, that is not always the case.

"We've had some people who can't go into certain rooms," Mary told me. Some tourists have felt a presence in certain rooms, and they were too afraid to go any farther. "They have to stand outside." Although Mary hasn't felt any threatening force in the house, Candace believes there is a reason some people do. "Hauntings exist because people leave their essence behind because something big happened."

"Something big" happened to John Cruikshank in 1924. "Mr. Cruikshank died here in the house in his bedroom," Mary said. I walked to his bedroom up the deep-red carpeted steps, pausing briefly on the second and third steps where Twain stood to give his speech. The bedroom was decorated in a turn-of-the-century floral pattern. The canopy bed John died on sits in the same spot it did in 1924. About a foot and a half of shaky scratch marks in the hardwood floor show all the distance it has been moved. The side where his spirit may—or may not—have passed over looks out upon the nearby river. "The mattress where he died has to be fluffed most mornings," Mary said. It has to be fluffed because it looks like someone has slept on it.

The day I was there, I saw the pattern a body might make in the mattress, but had a hard time photographing it. My auto-focus camera would not focus on the spot where Mr. Cruikshank died. "There's some rooms that the camera will not focus in," Mary said.

Photographers for *The Examiner* (a newspaper in Independence, Missouri, home to the Vaile Mansion and 1859 Jail hauntings), said the reason may be terrestrial—or not. "It could be that plain bed sheet doesn't have enough contrast for the camera to focus at that point," said photographer Paul Beaver. But Beaver's staff offered another reason. The camera could have picked up something between it and the bed. John Cruikshank maybe?

The second floor is also a gateway to another "active" room. "The ballroom on the third floor was the children's playroom," Mary said. "When you're on the second floor, you can sometimes hear the children running through the ballroom." A television news crew from Quincy, Illinois, once experienced problems while trying to broadcast from Rockcliffe Mansion. "They wouldn't believe what was happening," said Mary. "They were on the second floor and one of them yelled 'run.' They heard the children playing in the ballroom. They didn't know the things really happened here. They just thought it was something we talked about."

I didn't hear any children playing while on the second floor, but, then again, it was Saturday morning. Not the best time for ghosts. Red carpet covers the floor of the ballroom. The room is mostly empty—to leave room for dancing—except for sparse bits of furniture and the unexpected stone-faced mannequins in period dresses that silently stare from behind a security rope. They startled me. Those dresses tempted some of the high school tour guides into the ballroom in July 2005 ... for at least a few minutes. "We were looking up there for dresses and I turned around and there was this girl," said Paige Glascock, a former tour guide. "I was just dancing and ... she was looking at me and was holding up her dress and we just freaked out and ran." The other guides did not see the girl, but Paige didn't give them much of a chance. "I just turned around and I started screaming because that sort of stuff just freaks me out. And they started running." Paige's apparition was about fourteen years old, wearing "a long poofy kind of a dress. It was gray and had flowers. She had her hair up in a bun. She was just smiling. She just looked like she was happy." Paige didn't know if the girl eventually faded away or stayed for the next dance. "I didn't stick around to find out."

Apparitions, malfunctions, strange noises—they're all secondary to physical contact. "We had a young couple here who tried to go into the observatory, but something wouldn't let them," Mary said. "Something physically wouldn't let them in." The observatory atop the mansion, hot in the late morning, didn't offer resistance when I walked up the stairs to the little glass-encased room, just a nice view of downtown Hannibal and the Mississippi. But if there is a handsy spirit in the mansion, Mary should know about it. While she lived there, something unseen would let her know it was there. "I'd feel something brush by my hair. I'd turn around and no one was there. These things just happen."

Other people who work at the mansion, like Rhonda Brown Hall, have also had a few unexplainable moments. "I've encountered several ghosts in this house," said Rhonda, who has worked at Rockcliffe since fall 2004. "I experience things all the time because I'm the first one here usually and the last one to leave." She has felt a presence a number of times in the servants' hallway, but an emotional day brought something closer to her. "One day I was stressed and I was in the hallway and someone just touched me like 'it'll be all right.' It gets a little bit overpowering. It's not a scary feeling."

"I'm not sure I believe all of it," Mary said of the ghosts, "but there's something here." Candace agrees. "This is one house that has something extraordinary happening."

Rockcliffe Mansion

1000 Bird Street, Hannibal, MO 63401

Phone: 573/221-4140 (toll free 877/423-4140)
E-mail: info@rockcliffemansion.com
Website: www.rockcliffemansion.com
Mansion admission: adults $10; children, seniors $5
Ghost tours of Hannibal: $15
for information, go to tours.rockcliffemansion.com

Chapter 9

Lemp Mansion
St. Louis

Sticky air greeted me as I stepped onto the third floor of St. Louis's Lemp Mansion. Dusty floors and unfinished rooms showed that the servants' quarters were last on the list of restorations to the 140-year-old mansion. An occasional piece of furniture stacked against a wall was another sign this part of the house was seldom used. I walked by an old dresser, wondering who had used it and what secrets had been hidden inside its drawers, next to shirts, socks, and maybe a fine pair of pantaloons. I didn't open any drawer—I would hate to have someone looking through my pantaloons. Sweat trickled down my back. The summer heat permeating the third floor made the air around me thick and heavy. The lack of air conditioning was as obvious as the words "Go back now" spray-painted in red along one

wall. The hall ran the length of the building. Halfway down the long hall-way, sweat still dripping down my face, I bumped into someone—too bad I couldn't see them. In the hall, dotted with the occasional door behind which the Lemp servants once slept, I walked into an area of cold deep enough to raise goosebumps on my arms and dry the sweat on my temples. Yeah, it was cold.

I stepped back and the heat rushed over me again. There was no air con-ditioning on the third floor. Mary Wolff, director of operations at the Lemp Mansion, told me that before I started up the steps. There was only... I stepped forward and again hit the wall of frigid air. But just past that two-foot spot in the hallway, the heat of a stuffy attic enveloped me again, sending rivulets of sweat down my back. "I'm sure somebody was very curious about you," said Betsy Belanger, director of St. Louis Spirit Search, who conducts ghost tours at the Lemp Mansion. "They're always very curious."

A curious ghost? Could be. *Life* magazine once named the Lemp Man-sion, a restaurant since 1977 and a bed and breakfast since 1985, one of the ten most haunted houses in America. "There are seven identifiable spirits in that house. At least seven," said Betsy. "There's others we can't ID."

The Lemp Mansion, built in the early 1860s and purchased by presi-dent of the Lemp Brewery, William J. Lemp, has more than its share of tragic deaths. First there was Frederick Lemp, who died at the mansion in 1901 under "mysterious circumstances." Then his father, William J. Lemp, shot himself. William J. Lemp Jr., killed himself there, too, in 1922. His son, William Lemp III, died of a heart attack in the mansion in 1943 when he was forty-two. The last tragic death was William Jr.'s brother Charles. "Charles, in his younger days, was a very happy, friendly type of guy," Betsy said. "As he got older he got sour on life. He had arthritis and bone cancer. By the time he committed suicide in 1949, he was pretty well a recluse. My theory is he was compelled to live in the mansion because of the spirits that preceded him in death," she continued. "His brothers and his mother are still in the mansion to this day." Mary says Charles's spirit is the most active—along with his dog. "Charles Lemp had a Doberman pincher dog he had shot before he shot himself."

Lemp shot the dog because he was afraid nobody would take care of it after he had killed himself. The dog is still around, taking walks around the mansion. Fellow ghost hunters Sue and David Kanoy from St. Louis came with me to the mansion. They sat downstairs at the bar and grabbed an iced

tea while I wandered the thirty-three-room bed and breakfast. But Sue wasn't comfortable. "It was a warm day, and I noticed the inside of the house was really stuffy," Sue remembered. "I was wearing shorts and I sat on a stool and turned around. While I was sitting there, I felt something really cold brush up against my leg." She asked Dave if he had felt anything. He hadn't. "There was something really cold that hit my leg," she said. "Later…they told me there was a dog."

Charles' dog has kept guests up at night. "This guest said 'Was there a dog in here last night?' I said, 'No,' " Mary reported. "She told me, 'I could have sworn I heard a dog's claws on a tiled floor.' " The floors are carpeted, but they were originally hardwood. Clacking claws aren't all guests have heard. "There have been bed and breakfast guests who heard barking inside the house," Mary said. And then there's Charles.

"Charles, when he appears as an apparition, is usually in a business suit," Betsy said. "He has some shiny shoes and a very shiny bald head." Sometimes he wears a cape, sometimes a top hat. "A bride and groom said they had an uneasy feeling and awoke and saw an outline of a person at the end of their bed with a top hat on," Mary said. "As quickly as they could focus, there was no one in the room." A former resident of the mansion reported seeing that same apparition four decades ago when the building was a boarding house. "He had a top hat, cape, and shiny shoes," Mary continued. "In 1975, when my father purchased this building, we got a letter from someone in Arkansas [who] says he saw a ghost in the mid-'60s [when it was] a boarding house. He said he was going down the hallway late at night and saw a top-hatted figure with a cape on the stairs. He noted he had really shiny shoes." Then the man vanished.

Walking through the mansion with its Italian marble mantle, mahogany trim, and a hand-painted ceiling, I wondered what kind of people would have lived like this, and why suicide in the family was so prevalent. Why did the Lemps—some of the richest people in America—want to die? And, why did they die and then not leave? Cold spots, spectral dogs, and apparitions weren't the only evidence something else was in the house. Other guests have reported moaning from the chandelier area of the William Lemp suite, even though there are no rooms above that. They have also heard thuds, as if someone is kicking the bedroom door.

"The Lemp family was quite wealthy and the children were lazy," Mary said. "William Lemp, to get them roused, would kick the door." Maybe he still kicks it, trying to rouse his lazy kids. The couple who heard the kicking rushed to the door and looked to see who was screwing up their $175 a night stay. "There was a large tapestry in the stairwell that was flapping in the breeze," Mary reports. However, the windows weren't open and "there was no forced air in the building."

Employees have heard pianos play with no one there and have discovered lit candles in a banquet room that was dark just moments before. "It's a big place," Mary said. "You may think there's no one here, but someone may be playing a prank. But most of our employees are long-term. The ghosts haven't run too many people out." Apart from the Lemps, Betsy has sensed the ghosts of a servant who still cares for the spirit of a sixteen-year-old named Zeke, and a child named Elizabeth. "She's small, only nine to ten years old, and her communication skills are very limited," Betsy said. "She's afraid and looking for an answer."

But do a history of suicides and tortured spirits hurt the business at the family mansion turned restaurant and bed and breakfast? "It helps in the bed and breakfast area, but it doesn't really translate into the banquets and restaurant," Mary said, telling me the prospect of running into a ghost is too much for some people. "That deterred [a couple] from wanting their wedding reception there. They thought it would be bad luck. It's kind of a double-edged sword. When they ask if it's haunted, I say, 'Do you want it to be?' " But if you're looking for spirits, Betsy claims there are no bad locations in the Lemp Mansion. "Every single room in that house has spirits in it," Betsy said. "Not all at the same time. The majority of the time people feel something is on the third floor. That's the area where we have more encounters."

Yeah, tell me about it.

Lemp Mansion

3322 DeMenil Place, St. Louis, MO 63118

Phone: 314/664-8024
Website: www.lempmansion.com
Tours: Mondays at 7:30 PM, $15. Reservation required, call 314/776-4667 (tours not recommended for those under 16).

Chapter 10

Vaile Mansion
INDEPENDENCE

The Vaile Mansion, sitting in a residential neighborhood of Independence, is an elegant tribute to Victorian architecture, but the mansion has a murky past. Cecelia Sophia Vaile killed herself there on Valentine's Day in 1883. Doctors performed lobotomies on the insane within its walls. The house is also said to be the home of a ghostly woman in red who stands at the second floor staircase. Is she waiting for someone? A thin layer of clouds covered the waning moon above the Vaile Mansion as I approached. The mansion is neck-craningly high, brick walls stretch to ornate cast iron railings circling the roof. The windows were dark. Something could have been watching me, and I wouldn't have know it. Cool.

Harvey Merrick Vaile and his wife, Cecelia, moved into their newly-built

home October 12, 1881.
Harvey, who made his for-
tune running mail from St.
Louis to points west, was
quickly in trouble with the
law. "By December 1882, he
and his three partners were
indicted for mail fraud,"
said Sandy Dougherty, president of the Vaile Victorian
Society, a volunteer group
that cares for the mansion.
"That's what gave rise to
a great scandal." Having a
husband in trouble for mail
fraud presented many problems for Cecelia Vaile. "She
was more or less ostracized
from Independence soci-
ety," Sandy said.

Harvey went to Wash-
ington DC for the trial, but
Cecelia couldn't take the dis-
grace any longer. "While he was there, she overdosed on morphine," Sandy
said. "It was generally agreed upon that she committed suicide." The maid
found Cecelia lying in a second floor bedroom the same day a federal court
found Harvey not guilty. He came home to an inquest on his wife's death. "It's
a pretty sad story no matter how you tell it," Sandy added.

Inside, with the lights on, the Vaile Mansion doesn't look haunted.
It looks like a house Laura Ingalls Wilder was never invited to because
she was too poor. Original marble fireplaces are just part of the scenery
in the first floor rooms. Dark, heavy furniture, dominated by a massive
ornate mirror in the entry hall, made it look like I had stepped back into
the 1880s. But I wasn't there to tour the place. The carved wooden staircase
leading up to the floor where Cecelia Vaile committed suicide 120 years
ago was built from trees on the Vaile property. A full length mirror at the
top of the stairs reflects lights and shadows, giving the impression someone

else was there. Maybe someone was. This is the staircase where a figure has been seen by volunteers and tourists. "There was a lady on the staircase," Sandy reported, telling what others had seen. "It was very vague, but it had on a long dress."

The second floor, much like the first, is decorated in Victorian pieces. Ribbons draped over furniture let visitors know where they are not welcome. I headed for the bedrooms. "Everything that's happened to me has happened in the master bedroom or in Mrs. Vaile's bedroom," said Nadine Denn, a longtime docent at the mansion. "I went up one time and a voice said, 'Don't come in. I'm not ready.'" Nadine said she looked into the room, but no one was there. "She said her name is Rebecca in a soft, normal voice. It's happened two other times. Rebecca talks to me. 'I'm here now,' and things of this sort." But no one knows who Rebecca was. With so many people dying in the Vaile Mansion over the years—Cecelia Vaile, Harvey Vaile, and numerous mental patients—it may be impossible to tell. But Nadine has not only heard Rebecca, she may have seen her. "I was in Mrs. Vaile's bedroom dusting the mantle, and looked in the mirror and saw an apparition in the master bedroom," she said. "Just a white film swaying kind of thing. Smoke-like, you would say. I just said hello. What else would you do?" The apparition did not respond.

"For me, everything has happened in the upstairs bedroom area," Nadine continued. "When we're in the master bedroom, I usually try to tell what I know about Mrs. Vaile. When I forget to tell people this and I turn to leave, I get cold chills. It's like she is beckoning me back. 'Tell my story. Tell my story.' Yes, it has to have been her." Unlike Nadine, Sandy has never heard or seen anything unusual in the mansion. But she has spoken with visitors who have. "One lady refused to go into the Vaile's bedroom because she could feel such terrible cold emanations," Sandy said. "She kept going on about Mrs. Vaile being such an unhappy soul."

The second floor, much as the first, was quiet and, as far as I could tell, ghost-free. I went on to the third floor. After Harvey Vaile died in the house in 1894, his will was contested in a court battle that ended with Carrie Mae Carrol purchasing the Vaile Mansion for one dollar. Carrol tried to run it as an inn, but that failed. In 1901, she tried to sell spring water that was drawn and bottled on the property—"Vaile Pur Spring Water." That business failed too. During this time, she married a doctor and, in 1910, they turned the mansion into a nursing home for mental patients, most of whom were locked on the third floor. This was during the 1930s when doctors performed lobotomies on the insane. "The Vaile became infamous," Sandy said. "The third floor—a lot of heartache went on on that floor."

The state closed the nursing home in 1981. The third floor is still sectioned off into haphazard rooms where mental patients were kept—caged, in some cases. A door with a wire window still remains. "A number of times I have taken groups in what used to be the surgery room," Nadine said. "And a lot of people are like they've hit a brick wall and said, 'I'm not going in there. Bad things happened in there.'"

I didn't feel anything on the third floor, but I did smell something. One room, unrestored, still smelled of the urine that had soaked into its floor during its years as an asylum. It was around midnight, and I had experienced nothing paranormal. After an empty trip to the basement, I went back to the second floor for one last chance at a good spooking. The lady in red wasn't standing on the staircase as I walked up to the second floor. Rebecca wasn't calling me, and a smoke-like form wasn't reflected in the mirror of any bedroom. I sat in a chair without a "don't sit here ribbon" in the second-floor hallway. My guides shut out all the lights, and I waited for something to happen. It did—I got sleepy. I heard cars pass on the street outside. I heard my chair creak as I shifted my weight in an effort to stay awake. And I heard my stomach growl. But that was it. There were no rattling chains, no wailing moans, and no haunting laughs. As far as I could tell, the ghosts were playing hooky.

"I'm leaving," I said to the second floor in my outdoor voice. "If there's anyone here, I'd like to see you. Please show yourself." I waited a few seconds—nothing haunted floated by. But Nadine is convinced there's something ghostly in the Vaile Mansion. "I'm a Christian," she said. "And the Bible says don't call up the spirits, but too many things like this happen to tell you something else is out there."

Vaile Mansion

1500 North Liberty Street, Independence, MO 64050

Phone: 816/325-7430
Website: www.vailemansion.org
Tours: by request

Chapter 11

Big Cedar Lodge
RIDGEDALE

At dusk, Table Rock Lake glows like God threw fistfuls of silver dollars on its waves. Tree-covered hills obscure the vastness of this man-made 43,000-acre lake, and the college-campus size of Big Cedar Lodge. From a second floor balcony, I saw a young couple walking hand-in-hand on a lighted trail pause to kiss. They didn't see me—they had more important things to do. A boat puttered its way into a distant dock, too far away to destroy the peace of this green, brown, and blue Grant Wood evening. Sure, this Ozark night is like a good nap—but hopefully not for everyone. At least not, I hope, for Big Cedar's permanent guest, Dorothy Worman. I was staying at the lodge and I was looking forward to meeting her.

"Rumor has it she was unhappy here," said Shari Beckley, marketing manager at Big Cedar Lodge. Dorothy married young and lived in a secluded home her retired railroad tycoon husband Harry built for them in the 1920s. "At one point, she wound up going to Mexico and mysteriously

died," Beckley said. "He brought her back and scattered her ashes behind the Worman House." There her ghost may remain— and she is apparently not too happy about it.

"I think she's just a restless spirit or she wouldn't be here," said Willie Slaght, who worked the reception desk for thirteen years. "She's not scary. A little mischievous, but not scary." Willie has had a number of experiences with Dorothy. A little unexplained noise here, a little moving shadow there. But those were nothing compared to the night Slaght couldn't go home because of bad weather and stayed at the lodge. "I used the deadbolt," she said. "I went to bed late. I woke up early, which isn't like me. I looked over at the other bed and it was tore up like somebody slept in it. And it wasn't like that when I went to bed. She just wants people to know she's here and she's part of Big Cedar, but she'll kind of shock you."

The Worman House is only a few minutes south of Branson, but in 1920, long before Branson became the family entertainment getaway of the Midwest, Dorothy's house sat in the lonely Ozark woods. The house is

small compared to the 247-room Big Cedar Lodge complex. There is a sitting room and living room in the old Worman House, but, although the building has served many different purposes since Dorothy died, there is no kitchen. That doesn't mean anything to Dorothy. "When the Worman House was the reservation area, not a restaurant, the night auditor heard pots and pans rattling around and there were no pots and pans in the building," Willie said. I didn't hear pots or pans rattle and I didn't see weird shadows, but I wouldn't have minded hitting a cold spot or two since I had forgotten my deodorant on the trip. "There are so many people who feel her presence," Beckley said of guests. "Doors slamming, and on the back of the registration room there's a deck and a rocker will start rocking. There's no one in it, there's no wind, and it's the only one."

I walked the deck of the registration building and sat on one of the chairs, the softly bobbing waters of Table Rock encouraging me not to slam anything. Dorothy didn't join me on the deck. When the Worman House held the registration desk, Dorothy was much more personable. Betsy Gromowsky of Independence felt something unexpected when she and her husband stayed at Big Cedar on October 30, 1996. "I thought I was alone standing in front of the registration desk, and I just remember feeling a bump or a shove," Gromowsky said, "but it was accompanied by almost an electrical shock kind of feeling across my back." Then Gromowsky heard a woman's voice say "excuse me." "I twirled around and I was alone. I just had this incredible feeling of sadness and I began to cry."

Finished with the Worman House and the registration desk, I went to my room. The rooms at Big Cedar Lodge are decorated like a hunting lodge, with stone fireplaces, wooden furnishings, and the beady little eyes of stuffed raccoons, opossums, fox, and deer trophies staring through you while you sleep. Of course, the trophies might not be your only night visitor at Big Cedar. "I've had several guests tell me Dorothy had been in their room," Willie said. "One couple told me she was sitting at the end of their bed." I woke up a few times during the night. The raccoons were staring at me, the hawks were staring at me, but there was no strange woman staring at me. Probably for the best. My wife would have been ticked.

Employees and guests have seen Dorothy walking strolling across the lawn of the Worman House, wandering through the gift shop, and relaxing in the Devil's Pool Restaurant after hours. The description is always the same—a woman with long black hair wearing an old-fashioned white gown. Dorothy has even been known to sneak into pictures. "I had a couple come into the bar for their honeymoon and they wanted to have their picture taken in front of the bar," said Diane Bell, server in the lodge's Devil's Pool Restaurant. "They brought the picture back, and Dorothy's hair and silhouette was with them in the mirror. If I wouldn't have seen it, I wouldn't have believed it." Gromowsky believes it. She took a similar picture herself. In the picture was her friend bartending at Devil's Pool…and a woman with long black hair wearing an old-fashioned white gown.

Mary Tucker, who's worked at Big Cedar Lodge for four years, just thinks Dorothy wants attention. "One of the girls who worked here was cleaning and saw Dorothy in the mirror, with long flowing hair and a long white dress. I think she just wants you to know she's here."

Big Cedar Lodge

612 Devil's Pool Road, Ridgedale, MO 65739

Phone: 417/335-2777
E-mail: bigcedar@big-cedar.com
Website: www.big-cedar.com

Chapter 12

Grand Avenue
Bed and Breakfast
CARTHAGE

Albert Carmean does not greet everyone when they come to the Grand Avenue Bed and Breakfast in Carthage. He didn't greet me. But I guess I didn't expect to see him at this time of day anyway—he usually doesn't arrive until dark. I parked in front of the 1893 Victorian home at 1615 Grand Avenue, strolled up the walk, and rang the bell. No one came to the door, but I was early. I set down my bags and relaxed in a chair on the breezy wraparound front porch, watching neighbors mow their lawns and waving at kids walking home from school. Soon, owner Jeanne Goolsby arrived, her son Matthew licking the mint chocolate chip ice cream from the cone Jeanne had bought him after school. She let me in and showed me my room. I didn't see any evidence of Albert being home. But Albert doesn't usually let people know he is there until evening, when he lights a cigar and

lounges in the sitting room. It was only 3:00 PM. I had plenty of time.

Albert bought the late-Victorian mansion from its builder, S. H. Houser, after Houser declared bankruptcy. Albert was once an important man in Carthage: bank chairman, circuit court clerk, mine owner, and hardware store owner. He died on July 12, 1933, after a two-month illness. But just because he is dead doesn't mean he is not home. "One day when my husband was out of town, my daughter and I smelled cigar smoke," said Jeanne, "I went upstairs and it stopped at the landing. The next day I told my neighbor and she said, 'That's your ghost. He used to sit downstairs and smoke cigars.'"

Dee Eigenmann already knew about the smell when Jeanne approached her. She had heard about the cigars from a previous owner of the bed and breakfast. "She told me now and again you can smell a cigar in the old

room that was the old parlor in the house," Dee said. "She would smell that pretty often. When Jeanne moved in, she smelled exactly the same [odor] as every owner who's lived there. I've smelled the cigar smoke in her house. And when Jeanne called me and asked if I've been burning something, I said no. But I told her what [the previous owner] told me."

Jeanne brushes off the experience. "I've just been a chicken about things like ghosts. So I don't even like to talk about it." But Dee has experienced more than just the smell of cigars. "In Jeanne's house there are places for no reason at all I'll go completely cold. And I'll go to another room and it'll be gone," Dee said. "I think there's something in there, but I don't think Jeanne agrees with it or believes in it. I find it very interesting. You need to believe ... to experience things like that."

Roberta Williams of Carthage grew up in the home and, though she can't say she has met Albert, she did say there was something odd about the house. "I was seven when we moved there. We had it for a little over thirty years," Roberta said. "You could hear—when you were in the basement—you could hear whispers. You couldn't make out what they were saying, and there wasn't anyone else at home. But other people heard it too."

Jeanne and Michael Goolsbys have owned the bed and breakfast since 1997, and they have not heard the whispers or felt the cold. "As a full-time resident for the past eight years, it's just not part of my belief system," Michael said. "We just really enjoy old houses, and it's a way to make money owning an old house. We meet a lot of nice, interesting people." Some of those nice, interesting people have met Albert. "Jeanne might not like to talk about it. But some guests of the bed and breakfast do." So Jeanne has heard the stories. "Guests have said their lights have gone on and off and one thought she had seen someone," Jeanne said. "But it wasn't anyone in the house. They were all present and accounted for." Of course, there are those who have come to the bed and breakfast and struck out. "We've had people come here trying to find ghosts and they've never found anything."

I hoped that wasn't going to be my luck. I wanted to be like Corky Simpson, a writer with the *Tucson Citizen*. He and his wife were staying in the Louisa May Alcott Room when a visitor showed up. "I woke up one night, and I'm not pulling your leg," Corky began. "I thought, geez, I'm looking at a streetlight, but I don't remember there being a streetlight out there. I went to go back to sleep and the light didn't go away." That's because there is no streetlight outside the windows of that room. I know. That is the room I reserved for my night at the bed and breakfast.

But Corky saw something more than a light. "I saw the outline of this guy who had a cigar," he continued. "It wasn't a frightening thing at all. It was like a person with backlighting. He seemed to be an older fella, and he was smoking a cigar. It seemed to me like he had a derby or something, but I couldn't tell. It had the vague outline of a very high collar—something that would have been worn at the turn of the century. The most amazing part to me is that this wasn't something that frightened you. It was just there. You had a sense of serenity. It was like meeting some pleasant old guy in a bar. I thought, my God, am I dreaming this, or what's going on?"

Then Corky went back to sleep. The next morning at breakfast, he found out it wasn't a dream. "I did not bring this up, someone else did," Corky said. "She says, 'Do you guys have a ghost here?' When Jeanne said yes, my wife and I looked at each other and couldn't believe it. That's my story, and I'm stickin' with it."

I was going to put Corky's experience to the test. I settled into the Alcott room, a comfortable room on the second floor with white wallpaper sprinkled with pink flowers. I was ready to meet Albert. By the next morning, I had experienced no cold spot, no whispers, no cigar smoke, and no glowing, ghostly entity with a derby. I had, however, gotten a good night's sleep. "We've had other guests who've heard footsteps in the hall when they knew they were the only people in the house," Michael said. "[But] the more you want to see something, the less likely you'll see it." I guess so. I really wanted to see Albert, and I had come up short. But, then again, so has Michael. "The previous owner said that she was aware of a presence. I have not personally encountered it," Michael said. "We've never actively pursued the haunted aspect of our bed and breakfast, but we don't mind people thinking it is."

I think the house is haunted. Not from what didn't happen on my night's stay, but from something that happened a few weeks earlier. My wife and I visited the Grand Avenue Bed and Breakfast to take photographs. I had taken photographs of the sitting room—no Albert. I had taken photographs of the grand staircase—no Albert. And I had taken photographs of the Louisa May Alcott Room—no Albert. But going down the well-used walk that led to the street, my wife stopped me. We were standing on the end of the walk, just as the owner of the house would do if he were waiting for someone to come home.

"Do you smell that?" my wife asked. Yes, I did. It was tobacco smoke. We walked slowly back toward the house, and the smell of tobacco disappeared. We went through the grass toward the street, avoiding the end of the walk, but didn't smell smoke. Then, when we stepped back onto the last section of concrete, we were greeted by the smell of burning tobacco. Somebody was telling us good-bye.

Hi, Albert. Nice to meet you.

Grand Avenue Bed and Breakfast

1615 Grand Avenue, Carthage, MO 64836

Phone: 417/358-7265 (toll free 888/380-6786)
E-mail: reservation@grand-avenue.com
Website: www.grand-avenue.com
Tours: available by appointment

Chapter 13

1069 Salon and Spa
ST. CHARLES

When I pulled into the parking lot of the 1069 Salon and Spa in St. Charles, stylist Terri Dillick was pacing as she talked on her cell phone. Her black skirt flittered in the still air as she turned to face me. I would have made a defensive move too. Guys who wander around parking lots are kinda creepy. "Hello," I said, feeling a little guilty for interrupting her phone call. "I'm here to talk about ghosts." "Oh, yeah," she greeted me, the phone still stuck to an ear surrounded by a tight web of blonde hair. "There are some stories here." Terri had a story. I would talk with her later.

I followed Terri up the back stairs of the salon and into the ninety-nine-year-old building. The white, brick-front building was two stories high, bright, and full of windows.

Maddie Donovan met us in the waiting room and Terri handed me off, walking a client toward her station. A man sat in one of the waiting room chairs. I waited as Maddie welcomed a few more clients. The stylists walked back and forth between the cash register and their stations. They all looked like they just stepped out of a Diet Pepsi commercial, which is probably why a couple more guys walked in while I was there and sat down, happily awaiting their haircuts.

Maddie smiled as she handed me a history of the building. She had been waiting for me. When I talked with Maddie on the telephone two days before, she had told me something strange was going on at the salon. Maddie, her dark hair and tattoos a contrast to all the blonde heads and fair skin in the building, said she doesn't need to bring up the strange goings on to her clients—they bring it up to her. "My clients sometimes come in and they say, 'Did you know it was haunted?'" she began, "because they Googled it." The first two results from Google for "1069 Salon" are entries from a local paranormal research group—one the results of a 2005 investigation, the other a ghost story.

But Maddie doesn't need the Internet to tell her the salon is haunted; she's experienced something here too. "I've been here by myself and I thought it was the weirdest thing. It sounded like someone was on the stairs." The spiral stairs lead to the second floor loft, which holds a tanning room and the owners' office, and seems to be the center of strangeness—including the footsteps Maddie heard. Stylist Shannon O'Day has also experienced some of the mysteries of the loft. "I was here after hours with a friend and we both heard a whimpering, like a crying, coming from the loft and we were the only people here," she said. With two people in the building, at least one of them went upstairs, right? "No," she said quickly. "We ran out. It was scary. It was after hours. It was dark."

Other employees have heard footsteps from the loft when they were in the building alone, and stylist Jennifer Bongner has had problems with the lights. "I've closed down, left, and driven by here two hours later and the lights were on," she said. "And I knew I turned it off." Salon co-owner Karen Nowack knows the light problems have nothing to do with the wiring. "It's an old house, but all the electricity was redone," Karen said. She and Sharon Terbrock have owned 1069 Salon and Spa for "four years and a couple of months." Karen worked at the spa as a stylist for seven years before that.

Karen took me up the stairs—you can see the tops of a lot of heads from the loft. She told me that "a group of local ghost hunters had investigated. They said rechargeable batteries were drained and they said something electromagnetic flashed in the loft. They got orbs in pictures." Orbs, many believe, are ghosts captured in digital pictures.

I walked around the small loft, snapping pictures, and hoping for an orb or two myself. I had captured only two orbs during my own ghost investigations, each accompanied by a feeling of dread so severe I had to leave the area long before I had intended to. I didn't feel anything ill in the loft. Maybe the ghost was somewhere else, or maybe the aromatherapy candle was just a little too relaxing for me to feel too bad about anything. "I don't feel like anything evil's here," Karen said. "I only got weirded out one time. I was here at night and I don't know why."

On the first floor, plastic bottles of shampoo and conditioner fall from shelves for no apparent reason, objects move, and equipment comes on when no one is near it. Maddie said a hair dryer has come on when she was the only person in the building, and so has the radio. Of course, the radio coming on isn't that big of a shock compared to the fact that it also changes stations. Then there are the stylist's chairs. "When you push up the chairs, they lock in place," Shannon explained, motioning toward the shop. A former employee had pushed side-by-side chairs into that position one night when something odd happened. "She heard my dryer come on, and when she turned around to turn it off, the chairs were facing each other."

"I wish these things would happen to me," Karen said.

Karen doesn't know why the building may be haunted but there are hints in its history. The building was originally a home; Matthew and Mayme Peppard from Minnesota moved into it on May 28, 1907, shortly after it was built. The third owners, Basil P. and Elizabeth C. Elder, lived in the home from December 24, 1913, to August 3, 1921. Their son, Ezra W. Elder, was living in the house with his parents when he died in 1918 at the age of eighteen, but Karen doesn't know if Ezra died in the home.

"We're not sure," she said. "Two people died within two weeks of each other, too. We don't know if they died here." Those two people were Lula Olson, who died on November 27, 1983, and her husband Theodore H. Olson, who died December 9, 1983. They had lived in the house since 1942. But ghosts experts, like psychic Joyce Morgan of Miller Paranormal, don't think a person has to die in a house for his spirit to haunt that house. Morgan said ghosts "come in and out by their wish." Maybe Ezra, Lula, or Theodore come and go from their old home, and maybe, just maybe, they like messing with people.

"When I first opened up," Karen started, leading me into the basement where the telephone line was installed, "the only guy who put in the phone, he freaked out and came upstairs. He wouldn't finish. The phone guy

wouldn't tell what it was." The break room is also in the basement. Karen said the battery of a ghost hunter's camera died in the break room and had charged back up by the time the hunters left.

She led me around the old basement where boxes of hair-care products were stacked on the floor, and walked me through a few rooms, one which held a washer and dryer. A stylist once heard the dryer door shut when no one else was in the building. If a ghost is in 1069 Salon and Spa, it must be pretty handy to have a resident spirit who does laundry. So, okay, the stylists at 1069 Salon and Spa have heard things, seen items fall from shelves, and have gotten the heebie-jeebies, but has anyone seen a ghost?

"We've never seen anything as to what the ghost looks like," Shannon said, though she has seen something odd in her four years at the salon— something she can't explain. Shannon motioned toward the center of the building, "Something dark shot by in this room here. A client said, 'Is this a bird?' I wasn't crazy because Kay saw it too. The only thing I've heard that sounded like human voices was that whimper. I've never heard anything else, thank God. That night put me over the edge a little bit."

Some stylists carry prayer cards. "I have one at my station," Maddie said. And others just make sure they scoot out the door as soon as possible. But none of the twelve stylists have felt threatened in the salon, though they have been a little freaked out. "I was here by myself, and I don't like to be here by myself," Terri said. At 10:00 PM on a winter night, it was dark and, on a night like that in St. Charles, not much noise was coming in from the street. "I was sweeping hair up and it sounded like music had come on upstairs. I had turned it off," Terri told me. "I tried to tell myself it was a car going by, but it wasn't the kind of music they'd play in a car." No thumping bass. No screaming, long-haired, tattooed lead singer. No hip-hop. Just a whole lot of Sinatra. Did she investigate? "Oh, hell no," Terri said. "I dropped the broom, and I was like, I'm out of here."

But that wasn't the only time Terri had had problems while closing the salon. "I'm making [a client's] appointment at the front desk," she continued. "And we heard 'bow, bow, bow, bow.'" Her client fell down the short steps by the appointment desk. "She fell...and we were out of here," Terri said. "She kept saying, 'Don't look back, don't look back.' I kept looking back." But she didn't see anything. "It seems like a lot of time it's the timing that brings it to the forefront." 'Timing' being when people are alone and the evening is bathed in darkness. Why would strange things happen then? Because a radio popping on for no apparent reason isn't scary when it happens at 10:00 AM.

I left before anything spooky happened to me. Not that I didn't try to experience something. I wandered in the basement, I wandered in the loft, I stood on the spot where Terri's client fell down the stairs. Nothing. But I may be back some day. The next time I'm in St. Charles, I may just need a haircut at 10:00 PM, when unseen hands turn on radios and hair dryers and something whimpers in the night....

1069 Salon and Spa

1069 First Capitol Drive, St. Charles, MO 63301

Phone: 636/947-1069

School Spirits

Favorite teachers, recess, apples, new friends, and young love. The happy memories of our school days remain with us forever. If we're lucky, we forget the embarrassments, the bullies, strict principles, and unrequited love. But some schools harbor tragedies that refuse to fade. A women's college torn by war, a gasoline explosion that rocks a residence hall, and a conductor's sudden collapse during a concert are events we can't forget, no matter how hard we try. Their memory lingers long after all the witnesses are gone; they become a part of the school spirit that continues after the students have gone home, and sometimes even after death.

Chapter 14

Mt. Gilead Historical Site
KEARNEY

Mt. Gilead School is white. Cloud white. Bone white. Tom-Sawyer-tricking-people-into-whitewashing-a-fence white. The 1879 building sits among a grove of trees just off rural Plattsburg Road northeast of Kearney, next to an 1873 church and a cemetery that marks the resting place for Union and Confederate soldiers, and Archibald Lincoln, a cousin of President Lincoln. And it's really, really white. Children learned reading, writing, and arithmetic on the upper floor (now an apartment), and older students studied harder lessons, like Latin and Greek, downstairs. A mounting block sits under a tree, long ago used by area children who couldn't get on their horses to ride them home without a boost. Of course, I'm not going to pretend I knew that was the purpose of the stone. Phyllis told me.

Phyllis Green, Mt. Gilead's schoolmarm, met me at the door dressed in a white lace blouse and long blue skirt—period clothes of the 1890s. Phyllis has worked at the Mt. Gilead site since 2000, giving a demonstration of

rural education in the late 1800s to third and fourth grade students from the Kansas City area. And she tries to keep the sessions as history-friendly as possible. "We suggest what the children should wear and what the children should bring in their lunch pail," mainly because Dr Pepper doesn't agree with the nearly 130-year-old hardwood floors. Original blackboards line the walls, interrupted only by windows and a map featuring the Louisiana Purchase. Reproductions of the 1890s *McGuffey Reader* are available for visitors to read. The original two-to-a-seat desks sport holes for inkwells, and show more than a hundred year's worth of graffiti. And on the schoolmarm's desk sits, yes, an apple.

"We have children come from all over, as far as Odessa and Olathe," Phyllis said. "My goal was to get it booked this last year every day of the week, which I did." About 1,500 school children visited Mt. Gilead in 2005, up from previous years. Phyllis gives the children a four-hour education of 1890s games, history, and handwriting. "I teach penmanship—the Palmer Method. This is the book they learned out of," she explained, holding up the small, soft cover textbook *Palmer Method Handwriting: Grades Three and Four.* She grinned and winked at me, "Today they call it calligraphy."

The original school was a log building constructed in 1835. During the Civil War, legend has it, teachers dismissed classes so the children could watch the soldiers march. Some of those soldiers are buried in the cemetery next door. One of them, James M. Burgess, died in the Battle of

Vicksburg. The brick Mt. Gilead Christian Church next to the school was built in 1873, replacing the original church that burned in 1862. The church and school have always had close ties. "The church people actually built the schools," Phyllis said. "They thought the grounds they built their churches on were hallowed, and they wanted their children to go to school on hallowed ground."

But can hallowed ground be haunted? Park Ranger Vince Wonderlich lived in the school's second-floor apartment for two years. He is convinced someone unseen walks the floors of Mt. Gilead School. On the day Vince moved into the apartment, a former tenant warned him about visitors in the night. "One of the other rangers helped me get moved in and he told me there's lots of weird and unexplained things that happen there. He lived there too," Vince said. "He was just saying there was like scratches on the wall and pingings on the windows, and things like that. I just thought he was trying to scare me. I was the new guy."

That night, while Vince was making supper, he heard something downstairs. There was a locked door at the bottom of the stairs, but on the second floor, the staircase just opens into the apartment. "I thought I heard someone walking up the stairs. I thought surely it was just the rangers trying to scare me," he began. "It got closer and closer, and I got behind the railing so they wouldn't see me, and I jumped out to scare them, and no one was there." He paused and laughed. "Whoa. I looked down at the bottom of the stairway and the door was open. It only locks from the inside, and you need a key. I'd definitely locked it." An 1890s teacher or custodian checking to see who was living in their school, perhaps?

The school was incorporated into the nearby Kearney School District in the 1940s and was shut down in 1946. Clay County acquired the site in the mid-1980s and restored the school in 1998. Phyllis said the people at Clay County Historic Sites have done a good job keeping the school historically accurate. "About four or five years ago, they had a reunion here and brought back a lot of folks who went here as well as a teacher who was still alive," Phyllis said. "The people who went to school here and a 96-year-old teacher said everything was the same in the school, except the stove was in a different place." But there are occasionally other unexpected changes at Mt. Gilead School—and they are not always appreciated. During a field trip at the school, Phyllis took the students, teachers, and parents from the school to the church for music class and was surprised at what she found when they came back. "I always lock these doors," Phyllis said, pointing toward the back of the room to the only way into or out of the building. "Nobody could get in until I got back. I came over and unlocked the door and came in, and I thought, 'I was going to erase that blackboard,' and the blackboard was erased. I said to the parents, 'Was that blackboard erased when we walked out of here?' and they said no."

Vince has heard a little girl's voice downstairs in the classroom. Maybe she was just trying to earn the favor of the teacher. But a couple of events Vince experienced were not indicative of a little girl. "Close toward Christmas, I'd bought some of those battery-powered lights for the windows. I got a bunch of them." But when he placed the first one in the window, there was an unexpected reaction. "It kind of shook a little bit and fell off. I figured it was an old place. I put it back," he said. "The next night I put one up in the window sill. It started shaking like the other one. It fell off, but it was more like somebody threw it. "Another person would have stopped there, but I kept on going. I put one on and it was off and the light was partly unscrewed," he said. The bulb had been screwed in before he placed it in the window—he had checked. "After that, I took them down. I figured what was there didn't like them."

Later, whatever inhabited the schoolhouse with Vince got a little too personal. "I heard these unexplained noises downstairs. It was like machinery and a human voice," he said. "I tried to turn the radio up louder to drown out the sound. But it got louder. Half an hour later I laid down to go to sleep. I remember I laid down on my side. Then I got hit on my side like a linebacker and it pushed me on my stomach. I was in that half stage when you're asleep but still awake, and I was hit in the shoulder." He moved a short time later, though not because of the unwelcome visitors. "I grew up in an old house in Iowa and it was haunted," he said. "An old lady died in the house. I'm kind of used to unexplained events."

Others have reported shadows walking by windows in the church and mysterious lights when no one is in the building; one ranger claimed he saw a Civil War soldier through a window. These activities toyed with the personal life of a ranger before Vince. "He said, 'My girlfriend won't even go upstairs anymore,'" Phyllis reported. "'I always deadbolt [the door] in the evening, but I always go check it before I go to bed and it's open.'" Phyllis grinned. "Some old maid schoolteacher's making sure she's not up there."

Across the yard is the church. The pews and pulpit in the brick church are original, the pulpit made from a four-poster bed. A delicate, arched, hardwood ceiling gives the building "perfect acoustics," according to Phyllis. The county rents the church for weddings, family reunions, and meetings. When we walked through the church, the pews, painted white at some time in their past, were pushed together from some recent event. The church was important to the area residents who once held services in parishioners' homes. One of the church's first pastors, Elder James Morris, who died in 1861, is buried in Mt. Gilead Cemetery. "They were closely knit to their religion and their Bible verses, and it shows on their stones," Phyllis said. Bible verses and hands clasped in prayer decorate most of the gravestones. But the cemetery's most noteworthy resident lost his stone years ago. "President Abraham Lincoln had a cousin who lived north of Liberty," Phyllis said. "Children like walking in a cemetery where a cousin of President Abraham Lincoln is buried."

The school, church, and cemetery were quiet the day of my visit—no ghostly experiences. Phyllis has heard many ghost stories about the site, but she didn't believe in ghosts until the day she saw the cat. "I got here early because I have lots to set up," she said. "Then I went over to the church and set it up. I came back and waited for the group to arrive. I sat and took a breath. I was upset. I had worn this brooch a week before, and I rarely did. But it wasn't until I got home [that I] realized my brooch was missing. I came back and we looked all over the grounds. Couldn't find it. Several days later, I'm sitting here waiting for the bus and I said out loud, 'Okay ghosts, if you're here, show me where my brooch is.'" Then she noticed a cat sitting by her car. She had never seen a cat at Mt. Gilead before. "We never have cats out here. I go outside to see this kitty," she continued. "When I get out there, the cat was nowhere to be seen, and where it was sitting was my brooch."

Mt. Gilead Historical Site

15918 Plattsburg Road, Kearney, MO 64060

Phone: 816/628-6065
Website: wwww.claycogov.com/text/parks/#mtgilead
Tours: Available upon request

Chapter 15

Roberta Hall, Northwest Missouri State University

MARYVILLE

Orange, gold, and yellow leaves crunched under my feet as I walked across the Northwest Missouri State University campus. I was heading for a sorority house called Roberta Hall. As I strode across the lawn, past grand brick buildings, some of the 1,300 trees on campus, and the occasional errant Frisbee, I briefly thought that the groundskeepers would probably have preferred that I use one of the many sidewalks, but the sound of dead leaves complaining at my feet went too well with the featureless gray sky of fall. Besides, the lady I was going to meet wouldn't have cared. She never left home.

Roberta Hall wasn't always a sorority house, and it wasn't always called Roberta. In the early 1950s, when Roberta Steel attended Northwest Missouri State College, the women's dormitory was simply called Residence Hall. Then there was the explosion. On April 28,

1951, a steel gasoline storage tank at the railroad tracks behind Residence Hall exploded, sending a fifteen-foot-long Y-shaped brace of steel crashing into the upper floors of the southeast corner of the hall. This caused a fire that could be seen seventy miles away. It injured thirty women in the building, four of them critically. One of those critically injured women was Roberta Steel. "Roberta was in the shower when the explosion hit," said Cathy Palmer, archivist at Northwest. "She wouldn't come out for help because she was naked. Her modesty kept her from saving herself." Roberta survived the explosion and fire, but a year and a half later, in December 1952, her mother, Carolyn Steel, sent a telegram to the university president and his wife: "Roberta passed away suddenly tonight from failure of the liver as a result of the explosion." Could Roberta's spirit have returned to the place she was injured? The place that bears her name? Many residents of Roberta Hall throughout the years have thought so.

Linda Beatty of Kansas City attended Northwest from 1984 to 1988. Her brush with something odd in Roberta Hall happened in 1987. "I was in one room on the first floor in Roberta Hall. And this was back in the '80s and there were two of us home at the time," Linda said. "It was a Sunday night. We were just lying there watching TV on my old 19″ TV and we heard the crickety old doorknob move. We thought someone was coming in, but nobody was coming in." Linda and her roommate told the person behind the door to come in, but no one did. The doorknob inside the room just kept turning. "I got frustrated and opened the door and there was no one there," she said. Then Linda turned the doorknob on the hallway side of the door. That doorknob moved. The doorknob inside the room did not. "Somebody was moving the doorknob on the inside." Was it Roberta Steel? Maybe.

Jane Costello, who died in September 2005, went to school with Roberta and thought the legend of the haunting was fitting. "She was lots of fun," Jane said in a summer 2000 interview for Northwest's oral history program. "I read in the paper sometime at Northwest that she was being credited with the scaring—the haunting of Roberta Hall—and I had to laugh because you know if anybody's going to do it, it would be Roberta. She had a really terrific sense of humor."

Some people who have lived in Roberta Hall do not find the haunting funny. Stephanie Costanzo, a member of the Phi Mu sorority, is one of those people. She has had a few run-ins with the ghost of Roberta Hall and has not enjoyed them. "When we first moved in in August it was really hot," she said. "About a week later our air conditioner wouldn't work. We'd just come back from a bike ride and my roommate said, 'Roberta, I'm freaking hot' and the air conditioner went 'wooooh' and then it came on. But it was in the off position." Roberta might have just been doing Stephanie and her roommate a favor, and that would have been fitting. Roberta liked to help people, according to those who knew her. Roberta cut girls' hair in the dorm, even putting a barber pole outside her room.

"She was just a sweet, quiet girl," said Irma Merrick, a roommate of Roberta's sister, Carolyn. Irma attended Northwest from 1945 to 1949 and, though she had graduated and was already in her first year of teaching at the time of the explosion, she had met Roberta and had even stayed in the Steel family home in St. Joseph. "[They were] very friendly people," she said. But they were also reserved. Roberta wanted to join the sorority Sigma Sigma Sigma, but her father wouldn't allow it. "I was a Tri-Sig, all her friends were Tri-Sigs, but her dad didn't believe in sororities," said Virginia Helzer, a friend of Roberta's, in a spring 2000 interview for Northwest's oral history program. "So she just never did join."

So, would Roberta's father approve of his daughter's name on a sorority house? A picture of Roberta Steel hangs in the main lounge of Roberta Hall, a picture Irma said doesn't look like Roberta. To some, like Northwest graduate Sarah Wayman, the picture is just a piece of history. To others, it's a little eerie. "It's this big picture over the fireplace," Stephanie said. "It's creepy. I don't go in there."

Sarah, who was a member of the Sigma Kappa sorority, graduated in 2005 and lived in Roberta Hall from fall 2002 to spring 2003. Although most of her experiences were flickering lights and out-of-place noises, she and her suitemates also experienced something they couldn't explain. "Anything wrong that happened was blamed on Roberta," Sarah reported. "We discovered one morning that, hey, we can't get in our bathroom. We called each other saying, 'Did you lock the door to the bathroom?'" They couldn't have, because the doors locked on the inside. "We blamed it on Roberta."

Towels falling off their racks, pictures falling off the wall, and stereos turning on by themselves are also blamed on Roberta. So are flying drawers. Amanda Root, past president of the Phi Mu sorority, lived in Roberta Hall for two years. In 2004, she experienced Roberta twice, once when she was alone. "I was looking in the mirror, getting ready, and I saw my roommate's drawer shoot out of the dresser, and it really kind of scared me," she said. "I turned and was like, 'What the hell was that?' I grabbed my bag and left." But the flying drawer wasn't enough to prepare her for an unwelcome late-night visitor. "I had gotten up because I'd heard someone walking around and I thought it was my roommate, but I looked over and she was in bed," Amanda said. "I hadn't encountered anything like that, but when I heard somebody walking around, it really freaked me out. Our floor is really squeaky. I was really scared. I put the covers over my head. It's a good experience, I guess."

Over the years, residents of Roberta Hall have tried to find a way to keep Roberta Steel at bay. "Some girls do the little thing at the door to keep ghosts out," Stephanie said. 'The little thing' is something the university frowns upon. "To keep Roberta out, they'd take an iron and burn a mark into the carpet. That was supposed to keep her away. Why it would, I don't know," Cathy Palmer said. "In the early '90s, they remodeled Roberta Hall and said you'd be fined x-number of dollars if you burned an iron outside your door."

But despite disbelief and despite branding a mark in the floor outside your door, the ghost of Roberta Steel creeps into every floor of the old Residence Hall. Her legend leaves marks of its own. "When I'm in the room, I feel this tingling on the back of my neck, and I get up and get out," Stephanie said. "I won't stay there alone—ever."

Roberta Hall, Northwest Missouri State University

800 University Drive, Maryville, MO 64468

NWMSU phone: 660/562-1212
Roberta Hall phone: 660/562-1408
Website: www.nwmissouri.edu

Chapter 16

Senior Hall, Stephens College
COLUMBIA

Senior Hall stands out among the five buildings on the historic quad of Stephens College in Columbia. And why not? It's the only one with a bell tower. I walked across the quad under a crayon-blue sky toward the 114-year-old brick building. I was looking for Sarah, the oldest student at Stephens. She probably is not the most famous Stephens student—that would be Dawn Wells (Mary Ann from *Gilligan's Island*)—but she might be next in line. No one rushed past me, late for class. No one sat in the drowsy shade of the quad's trees reading Tolstoy or *MAD Magazine* or whatever it is college students read these days. It was quiet. Maybe Sarah likes the quiet. Peter Byger, drama teacher at Stephens since 1971, found that out his first Halloween on the job. It had to be on Halloween. After all, Sarah is dead.

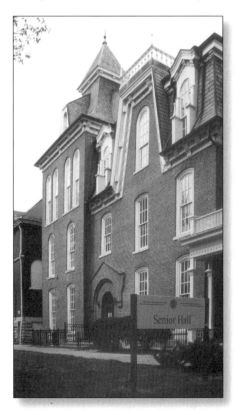

"I was at school at Stephens as an actor-instructor," Peter said. "I'd heard about the legend of the ghost of Senior Hall and I decided we would have a séance." Peter wanted to contact the spirit of Sarah Jane Wheeler, a young Southern girl who had studied at what was in the 1860s the Columbia Baptist Female College. The finishing school for Southern ladies had existed as one house that would later become Senior Hall. Although the cause of her death is contested by historians, ghost hunters agree it must have been tragic. A Confederate soldier, injured out-side Columbia during a skirmish between Union and Confederate troops, arrived at the college, injured, and begging for aid. "The girls heard him cry-ing for help, then they let him in and nursed him back to health," Peter said. Troops followed the soldier's trail of blood, but wouldn't enter the college grounds. "The girls would stand by the iron fence and they would taunt the soldiers. Whatever happened in that dorm must have been interesting."

During his recuperation, the soldier fell in love with Wheeler. But his-torians can't agree on which side the soldier served. "The lover was a Con-federate or the lover was a Union soldier," said Dr. Alan Havig, professor of history at Stephens since 1967. "She hid him, in any case. If he was Union, love can overcome political loyalties." Desperate to be together, the lovers tried to escape from the building, and somehow died. "It was a rainy night when they escaped," continued Peter. "The story was they drowned in the Missouri River. I don't think that's true. I think that's Hinkson Creek."

One popular legend says that Wheeler witnessed enemy soldiers hang her lover, so she threw herself from the bell tower rising from the third floor of Senior Hall. Students have visited the tower over the years, writing graffiti and probably playing with Ouja boards. The tower is locked now, but in the 1860s it didn't have to be locked to keep students out—the tower didn't exist. "There are lots of variations," said Alan, who doesn't believe in the ghost of Sarah Wheeler. "She either threw herself down the stairs or she jumped out of the tower or they threw themselves into Hinkson Creek or the Missouri River. There's no way to know if anything happened."

But Peter is sure something happened. Halloween eve 1971, Peter held a punch and cookies party in the downstairs of the aging building. Then he took his wife and a few students to the third floor's bell tower room for a séance. "We went up hand-in-hand and lit candles around midnight," Peter said. The group passed Bob M. Gassaway, a reporter for the *Columbia Tri-bune*, who was camping on the third floor for a Halloween story. "We went up the stairs and went in the room and sat down," he continued. "We put our candles on the floor and, at that point, the door slammed, the candles were blown out, and one of the girls in the group screamed and passed out, and we heard all sorts of commotion in the hallway. Everyone was kind of frozen there." Peter opened the door to find the reporter trying to get into the room. "And they said, 'Did you see them? Did you see them?' I said, 'Who?'"

The journalist reported a man in a gray uniform and a woman in a nightgown walked past them and disappeared down the steps. In his November 1, 1971, interpretation of the events, Gassaway wrote, "There was the sound of slow steps at first. When they stopped, deep breathing became audible. I waited for the person to come through the door. And waited. And waited. Finally I took the initiative, hauled myself off the floor and moved to the hallway's mouth. Halfway down the hall...I saw the figure of a man. Then the swish of a woman's long skirt caught my eye as the man dropped into a half crouch, his left hand outstretched as though to ward something off. Then both figures disappeared down the stairs—quietly."

Peter is still not sure what the man saw. "It could have been students, or it could have been a ghost," Peter said. "You don't know. It was Halloween eve." Peter made sure the students were okay, then they all went home. But Sarah Jane Wheeler wasn't finished with Peter. "I got a call about three in the morning. It was two girls coming back from a party and were passing Senior Hall. They met a woman in a gown and she told them I was no longer welcome in Senior Hall, but my wife was." The apparition mentioned Peter and his wife by name. "The two girls called me and they were hysterical," Peter said. "Still, to this day, I always feel a little strange going over there."

Alan isn't impressed by ghost stories. "In the '70s or early '80s, the building was more or less abandoned. A lot of students used to break in on Halloween night," he said. "They said they experienced sightings, but, of course, no pictures." The school restored and rededicated Senior Hall in the 1990s. It's now home to music and dancing classes, but the ghost stories persist. "I take the attitude that there are no ghosts. I think people dream these things up. There's an old building, a door slams, and it's a ghost. It's just something students adhere to. Colleges need that. Especially ones without football teams."

Senior Hall, Stephens College

1200 East Broadway Street, Columbia, MO 65215

Phone: 573/442-2211 (800/876-7207)
Website: www.stephens.edu

Chapter 17

Yeater Hall, University of Central Missouri

WARRENSBURG

It was 96 degrees the day I visited Warrensburg, a town where I had lived for four and a half years as a college student at the University of Central Missouri. Something was different. Was it the fast food joints and chain stores I never thought would make a stop in this mid-Missouri town? Was it the fact that I was there to visit a woman who had been dead for fifty-three years? Or, maybe it was because, unlike when I was a student here, today I was sober. Yeah, that's a big difference. But some things hadn't changed since I was a shave-once-a-week college freshman. As I stood across from Laura J. Yeater Hall on the campus of UCM, the red brick building sitting like an ancient ruin among the trees looked like it had not changed in seventy years. A single window loomed from the attic of Yeater Hall, overlooking the trees and glaring down at the lot where I sat. Twenty years ago, rumor was that something would stare at passersby from that window. I had never looked before now. Today I couldn't help

it. I was there to investigate the claim of generations of college students that Yeater Hall was haunted. Yeater is the oldest residence building on the campus of University of Central Missouri and, according to people familiar with it, is still home to the school's oldest resident.

Laura J. Yeater was head of the college's Latin and Greek department between 1901 and 1914, when the college was a teacher training school. She had pushed for women's housing on campus, and finally, in 1940, the college (then named Central Missouri State Teacher's College) constructed the three-story Yeater Hall with money she had helped to raise. In the decades after the dormitory opened, many students have reported mysterious footsteps, stacked furniture, blankets being ripped off beds, and strange lights in the dormitory. Did Laura, who died in April 1954, love the building that bears her name enough to make it her permanent home?

Vivian L. Richardson, assistant director of the university's museum/archives department, knows of the stories about Laura's ghost, but she doesn't put much stock in them. "I've heard what probably everyone's heard. Noises," she said. "Anyplace with a lot of people is going to have some ghost stories."

Alan Nordyke, director of Residence Life for the past thirteen years, met me at the entrance of Yeater Hall. The hall was closed during the summer, and the doors were kept locked. Custodial worker Carol Mullins was there to greet us. "It's a very old myth that Laura Yeater, her ghost, supposedly is here," Alan said. "I've never heard any encounter that couldn't be explained. I don't know if it's true or not true." But some people think the ghost stories may be true—including Carol. "I started here in 2001 and I heard a lot of stories and it was fun," she said, her voice lowering. "Oh, there are ghosts. The first three years I hadn't experienced anything that would convince me that there were ghosts here. But there've been enough the past two years to convince me something's here."

Sweat streamed down my face in the stifling heat inside the old brick dormitory. I'm sure students were happy they couldn't stay there during summer session. "It's the oldest [resident] building on campus," Alan said. "There's no air conditioning. If we had air conditioning in this building, it would probably be the most popular building on campus." Yeah, it was pretty enough. Hardwood floors ran through each room, windows looked out on either a tree-lined path or a spacious courtyard and, darn it, the building just felt elegant. Yeater Hall once housed sororities and banquets and, during World War II, soldiers awaiting transportation to Europe. But few of these things had to do with the third floor, where footsteps, scooting furniture, and unexplained lights have been reported from behind locked doors. Alan and Carol led me up the winding stairs to the third floor land-ing, where a metal latch and padlock sealed that level of Yeater from the rest of the world.

"It's closed because of electrical problems and the decline in occupan-cy," Alan said as he snapped open the lock with his key—one of a very few keys on campus that allow access to that floor. "The only people who'd have access are employees. Students don't have access." And if students gained access to the third floor … well, Alan threw out the word "trespassing" like he meant it. "The third floor is locked all the time," he said, opening the door, revealing a floor that was somehow even hotter than the rest of the building. "If someone were up here, it would be employees."

Carol has been to the third floor a number of times since she started working there in 2001. "In March 2001, the top floor was open and in use," she said. "That fall they closed it up. That next year they put the padlocks on. Something caused them to put the padlocks on." A few ceiling lights were on as we walked down a barren hall lined with doors opened to rooms that once housed co-eds. "I thought there were electric problems," I men-tioned as I followed Alan and Carol under the glow of those lights. "Some lights are left on," Alan said. Uh, okay … on an abandoned floor with elec-trical problems. Strange lights have been associated with the third floor of Yeater for at least twenty years. The room lights in 337 and 334 have been reported to pop on some nights after 10:00 PM for no apparent reason.

"The lights have been going on for twenty years," Carol said, pooh-poohing the possibility of the lights coming on by human hand. "Nobody's going to be doing it for twenty years." David Shewell, a junior criminal justice major at UCM, has been fascinated with the paranormal since his sophomore year in high school when he encountered the spirit of a girl in the basement of Roosevelt School in Excelsior Springs. He's investigated Yeater Hall on and off for about a year. "At first I didn't believe it and [then] I walked by Yeater one night at about 2:00 AM and there were two lights on," David said. "I asked university housing why the third floor was locked, and they said it was because of wiring problems throughout the building. If there's wiring problems, why did they just close the one floor?"

Alan and Carol walked by 337 on their way to an anomaly in 343, but I stopped to take a picture. Looking through the viewfinder of my Minolta, I

saw the ceiling light in 337 was on. I snapped the picture. "Uh, Alan, Carol,"
I said. "The light's on in this room." They came back. "This shouldn't be,"
Alan said, citing maintenance workers as possible culprits. He switched off
the light, then we walked to room 343, one half of a suite at the end of the
hallway. The suites were big, with their own bathrooms. But 343 held a mystery—a milky handprint on the bathroom window. The white, left handprint
of a large man stains the inside of a double pane of glass in the bathroom of
this suite. Standing on a chair and turning my arm, I realized the only way
this handprint could be there was if the person were 1) working at the factory
that made the window, 2) standing upside down on the ceiling with access
to the interior of the double pane, or 3) someone I didn't want to meet. The
handprint was a mystery, yes. But not as much as the lights.

"The light comes on when no one is here," Carol said. "I had [another
maintenance worker] lock the door and I duct-taped the light switch. When
I came back up, the doors were still closed, but they were unlocked. When I
went in, the duct tape was pried open to turn the light on." As we walked back
by 337, we stopped.
The light was on again.
The three of us had all
been in full view of
the only door into the
room and no one had
come in or gone out.
We were alone on the
third floor and, I think,
in the building. The
light switch Alan had
turned off was in the
on position. Accord-
ing to engineer Will
Murphy at Northwest
Missouri State Univer-
sity, that couldn't hap-
pen without a finger
involved. Was Laura
letting us know she
was watching?

Jessica Cross graduated from UCM in 2006 with a degree in management. She lived in 243 Yeater Hall for four years and is familiar with the light. "I've seen lights come on in the room. Not only that room but other rooms on that side of the wing," Jessica said. "The room light. It comes on and it turns off. They say it's an electrical problem, but if it was really an electrical problem, they would have the money to fix it and it would affect the rest of the building, which it doesn't. I just thought that was a pretty lame excuse."

A 2002 article in the UCM student newspaper reported that the university housing office's explanation for the padlocked third floor was simply that "[we] don't need the space." I don't know why the third floor is abandoned. I just know a light came on by itself. "Thank you, Laura," Carol said, grinning as she took a last look at the third floor before Alan padlocked the door again.

Katy Bird of Kansas City, a management major at UCM, lived in 219 Yeater Hall as a freshman in 2005, and knows strange things happen in Yeater Hall. "When I first moved in here, I started hearing the toilet flush above me," she said. "I later found out it was broken, so it was kind of awkward." Especially when she mentioned the flushing to her roommate. "I would hear the toilet flush. She wouldn't hear it, only me." But strange noises didn't stop at the commode. The sound of furniture pushing itself across the hardwood floor above her would occasionally creep into her room, and disembodied voices would make themselves known. "There were a couple of instances that I heard something and no one's been there," Katy said. "But you couldn't hear what they were saying. It was kind of mumbled."

Katy is not alone when it comes to hearing noises in Room 219. "There have been times when my roommate and I have stayed here for the weekend and my suitemates have left and we've heard their bathroom door slam a few times and we knew for a fact that they weren't there," she said. "That was kind of weird. We didn't really believe in the whole ghost thing when we moved here. But we're convinced there was something in the dorm. Things like that just don't happen."

Jessica Cross doesn't believe in ghosts, but she knows Katy is telling the truth. She and her roommate were both in bed around midnight when they heard something above that shouldn't have been. "The third floor had been padlocked and the attic had been nailed shut, so it's not like students could have gotten up there and played pranks," she said. "We heard all the furniture scoot into the middle of the room. The two dressers and the beds moved to the middle of the floor. It would have been a big person to move them. They're not like the dressers today. They're old and built heavy." Jessica and her roommate told Carol about the noise. "We were scared," Jessica admitted. "It didn't happen again after that. It just stopped. It only happened once."

Something unexpected happened to Carol in Yeater Hall only once. But once was enough for her. "On the ground floor we have a men's bathroom and a women's bathroom," she told me. "I was walking toward the men's bathroom and something came flying down the stairs to the women's bathroom. All I thought was, 'Wow that little girl had to go bad.' But I didn't see a head. I didn't see arms. I just saw a brown base. I thought, 'What was that?' Because it didn't look human." Didn't she go into the bathroom to investigate? "No. I wish I had," she said, "but I was too big of a chicken."

Rooms that once housed sororities are in Yeater's basement. So is the dormitory's original banquet room. Carol took me there, because that's where she occasionally plants a tape recorder to capture EVPs (electronic voice phenomena; audio recordings of voices in an empty room). "The ground floor of Yeater used to be a banquet room. It was huge," she said. "I put my tape recorder here. I picked it up the next day and there were like a dozen girls giggling outside the door. It was the summer. How were there girls giggling? Maybe it was from the past." David sees some validity in that. "At one point in the recording you start hearing a lot of chit-chattering of women," he said. "[Carol] and I were talking about it, and we came up with a theory that it was a lost memory of the building. That area was a big dining hall. Maybe there was a party. Maybe it was a lost memory." David has taken pictures of orbs in the basement of Yeater, and has seen a moving shadow he can't explain. He has also had the feeling he's not alone. "I get the feeling of being watched," he said. "One of the rooms I went into … I got light-headed. I don't know what was going on. I've gotten a couple of feelings that I've been watched."

Sweat hadn't stopped running down my face and back since I set foot in Yeater. As I stood in the basement with Carol, trying to wipe the sweat from my eyes, I wondered why I hadn't investigated this building earlier in the spring. Carol had just flipped open an album with a photograph of the lights on in room 337 when a cool blanket of air wrapped around me, erasing the heat of the mid-90 degree day and giving me a sudden, shaking chill. It felt like someone had turned on the building's air conditioning, but, as Alan had pointed out, Yeater had no air conditioning.

"Do you feel that?" I asked Carol. "What?" she asked. "That cold." She shook her head. I stood engulfed in cold for several minutes. The sweat on my face dried and the hair on my arms stood up. I kept looking through the photo album. The cold eventually dissipated and the sweat started dripping from my pores again. I smiled. I had come hunting ghosts, and they found me—twice. Yeah, something strange is going on in Yeater Hall.

"The few things I've seen, I think they could have been done by humans, but I don't know how," Carol said. "There's too many stories. Even though I love this building, sometimes it gives me the heebie-jeebies."

Yeater Hall, University of Central Missouri

Laura J. Yeater Hall, South Holden Street, Warrensburg, MO 64093

Phone: 660/543-4111 (main number)
Website: www.cmsu.edu

Chapter 18

Central Methodist University

FAYETTE

The knock came from the bathroom door. Megan Blair sat studying in her bedroom in Central Methodist University's Howard-Payne dorm. It was late, 12:30, maybe 1:00, on a warm, quiet night in early fall when she heard the noise—tap, tap, tap. Every five seconds—tap, tap, tap. And it stopped. Minutes limped by. One, five, ten, then . . . tap, tap, tap. Megan didn't slip the books off her lap and stand up. She didn't walk slowly toward the bathroom. She didn't try to quietly ease open the squeaky old dormitory door. She didn't have to. "No one was in there," Megan said. "That was enough to freak me out." Um, okay. Megan, a biology and economic science major at Central Methodist in Fayette, probably wouldn't have been too worried if whatever was rapping on her bathroom door had brought pizza. But the fact that she was in Howard-Payne made the knock something to worry about.

"Howard-Payne is where all the whacky stuff happens," said Melanie Schaefer, a former financial assistance counselor at the university and my tour guide for the day. One of a number of haunted sites on the Central Methodist campus, the How-ard-Payne dorm—marked out-side by a carved stone that reads "Howard Female College"—has a reason to be haunted. Suppos-edly, while the college was refur-bishing Howard-Payne in the

1940s, a brick fell and struck a student on the head, killing her, though details are sketchy enough to make the story sound like an urban legend. Since then, her spirit has been seen outside the dorm, but more typically her spirit has been experienced inside the building. A tap, tap here, a tap, tap there. …

"I was in my room all by myself and all of a sudden I heard that knocking on my bathroom door," Megan said. There was no way into or out of the bathroom except by that door. "At first I thought it was the pipes or something, but it kept doing that. It was clearly plain knocking," she said, rapping her knuckles on a wooden desktop. "Like that. I told myself, 'I don't believe in this stuff,' but I didn't sleep much that night." She didn't use the bathroom that night either—no matter how badly she needed to. "I did not go. I did not knock on the door. I didn't investigate."

And students who had lived in Megan's room in 2004 didn't say anything to soothe her fears. "They complained of knocking on the bathroom door," she said. Kristin Roberts is an assistant director in the admissions office at Central Methodist. She went to Central from 1998 to 2002, and graduated with a master's degree in 2005. As an undergraduate, she lived in Megan's room and had some experiences herself. "I never slept with the light off in the bathroom," she told me. "I left the door open overnight. I'm not afraid of the dark, but I wasn't ever comfortable there. When I first moved into this building, I'd have the lamp on and it would be off in the morning, the fish tank light would be off, and something would knock. It was an old building, and I tried to explain my way out of it." But knocking is only one of the anomalies at Howard-Payne. "Faucets come on," said Deontae Curtis, a student at Central. "Lights come on and go off. Toilets flush. There are strange sounds on the fourth floor on the ceiling. It was just a weird feeling up there."

Cara Cairer, residence hall director for Howard-Payne, said there is a reason noises may come from the fourth floor ceiling. "The fifth floor, they say a girl committed suicide and hanged herself," said Cara, who graduated from Central in 2001. "When I was a student here, this wasn't even open to students." The story of a suicide in the dorm was confirmed by the student paper, *The Talon*. Cara took me to the fifth floor. It's opened to students now, although few live there. "They've been anxiously awaiting something to happen and nothing has. I still don't like to be up here."

No one was home as we walked the fifth floor. Well, except for the guy in a towel. "Do you have any haunted stories?" Cara asked as he walked from the showers to his room. "Haunted?" he said. "Yeah, I guess." "Would you like to share your story?" I asked. He smiled and shook his head. "I'm in a towel," he said, and walked into his room. Rooms on the fifth floor are long and narrow, walk-in closets run across one wall, and pipes run across the ceiling. A perfect place for someone to hang themselves?

"I was always scared of the fifth floor," Kristin said. On a Friday the 13th in October during Kristin's junior year, she and a few friends were decorating a room on the fifth floor for a Halloween movie scare-a-thon when the room became uncomfortable. "It was so hot in this room we had the windows open, but we got hungry so we left," she said. "The door locks behind you, so that door locked and nobody [else] has keys to it. We go back up and the fan is off and the windows are down and it's so hot in that room we start baking. We kept all the lights on at the Halloween party that night."

Meghann Teague works with Kristin in the admissions office. She attended Central from 2001 through 2005 and she has also had problems on Howard-Payne's fifth floor. "I was on the fifth floor with Cara two summers ago," she said. "We went up there because [the boss] said all the windows were open and we had to shut the windows. Nobody had been in this building for a month. About ten rooms needed their windows shut."

Megan Witte, a junior who lives in Howard-Payne, has had her own experiences—mainly lamps going on and off—but

she knows whatever weird thing happens to her there, she's not alone. "Everyone who's ever lived here has experienced something," she said.

***

One of Central Methodist University's other ghostly residents, a former band director, is a little more visible. Jim Steele, owner and publisher of *The Fayette Advertiser* and *The Democrat-Leader,* was a senior at Central Methodist on May 1, 1964, the night of a band concert that left its note on the college. "Tom Birch was the band director," Jim began. Birch had graduated from Central Methodist in 1937, Jim told me, served in World War II, and taught music at a few schools, including the University of Missouri–Columbia, before he came back to Central, this time as a teacher "He was not very old," Jim continued. "He was fifty-two. Very nice guy. He took over as director [of] the Central Methodist Band around 1953 and had been on the job for probably a decade or so." And on the night of May 1, Dr. Birch gave his last concert.

"We had just returned for the annual spring concert, and I was tied into the band as a business manager with them," Jim said. "I was just a student." Birch was ready for the Friday night concert; the band would be playing Moussorgsky's "Pictures at an Exhibition." "It was kind of a warm pleasant spring evening," Jim said. "He had the white starched shirt, tails, the usual things. He was ready to direct the band." But during a selection in the piece called 'The Catacombs,' Birch had a heart attack. "Just as he had gotten into [The Catacombs] there was a 'whoo.' A gasp you could hear in the audience. He fell backward from the stage. He hit a platform in the well and fell into some drums set up for a number, and he fell onto the floor of the auditorium. He laid there gasping for several minutes. Eventually these death gasps became shorter. It was a terribly traumatic experience."

But, as relatively recent legend has it, Dr. Birch still spends time at the concert hall. On the clock tower where Melanie Schaefer says people have reported faces staring out of windows, there is a plaque that reads "Paul H. Linn Memorial, UMC—1932." Near that plaque is the entrance to the hall where Dr. Birch had pleasant memories and his last concert. It's also the spot people have reported seeing a man in a tuxedo smoking a cigar. A man who very much resembles Dr. Birch. The first time was in the 1970s, on a pleasant spring evening. ...

"A girl was going from the student union across campus to Cross Memorial Clock Tower on the campus's quadrangle," said Robert Bray,

Central's Alumni Director at the time of the incident. "The apparition appeared and said, 'Nice evening for a concert.' She went and got a boyfriend and went into the conservatory. She went into the band room and there's a picture of Dr. Birch, and that's how she identified him."

Jim said people talk about several significant sightings of Dr. Birch's ghost over the years, but he is not necessarily convinced the band director still waits outside the auditorium on a warm, spring evening for a concert he'll never direct. "The lore and the legend may grow out of proportion of what may have happened," Jim said. "I can't say. I've never seen the ghost, but I was present when he died."

N. Louise Wright, dean of the conservatory of music at Central, died in 1958 much like Tom Birch, during a performance, and some say her spirit still lingers. Others talk about the ghost of a stable boy who was killed at the site of Brannock Hall during the Civil War. Walking through the old brick campus, stopping at the tower, staring at the little windows looking for faces that never appeared, snapping pictures of the auditorium where Dr. Birch met his end, and poking my nose into closets where a young woman supposedly ended her life, I felt nothing out of the ordinary. But I came away from Central Methodist University with one solid impression: it would be fun to visit some of these places—alone, at night.

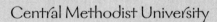

Central Methodist University

411 Central Methodist Square, Fayette, MO, 65248

Phone: 877/CMU-1854
Website: www.centralmethodist.edu

Ghostly Graveyards

Cold stones mark the final resting places of the dead, but they don't hold the dead in place. Sometimes the dead walk. And sometimes, so do the stones. Names, dates, and epitaphs—some weather-beaten, some crisp—tell visitors a short version of a loved one's life. Some mark a mass grave filled with the anonymous who wander in search of the families who left them behind. Other graves are stoneless, silent about those who lie below.

Chapter 19

Workman Chapel
M-ARYVILLE

Tombstones rise like broken teeth from the ground outside Workman Chapel. Pulling into the dirt drive from the gravel road that passes by the chapel, my headlights bounced off those stones in the tree-dotted cemetery. They are kept behind a black iron fence—though I didn't know if the fence was to keep something out or to keep something in. Either way, the rusty gate wasn't reassuring. The silence of the night grew oppressive when I turned off my car—there was no traffic this far out of town to disrupt my ghost hunting trip, though the occasional moo from a nearby pasture broke the noise vacuum that rested over the cemetery. The three-quarters full yellow moon lit the night, revealing the peeling white paint, and the empty, cavernous holes in Workman Chapel that used to hold windows

and doors. I'd heard enough about voices in the chapel and shadows that stalked the night to make me cautious. I needed to be cautious, I realized as I got out of my car and walked toward the chapel: in the moonlight I could see that parts of the floor were missing.

Something rattled against a spot on the wall next to my head as I stepped into the threshold of the church, sucking the breath from my chest, and throwing my heart into a speed I'm sure wasn't at all healthy. Probably a bird, or maybe a bat, I thought. Either way, I cursed. College kids love to play here, I saw as I stepped inside the church, crushed beer cans and broken bottles outnumbering the ghosts so far. Standing and letting my heart calm down, I gazed out the window at the tombstones glowing yellow in the fall moonlight and waited for something to happen.

John Workman built the chapel in 1901. His descendent Lester Workman is caretaker of the chapel and cemetery. He lives about a mile and a quarter east of the chapel. "It's been empty for years," Lester said of the chapel. "I've lived here fifty-six years. It's been fifty years or better. I [had] just moved up here to the community and went to one or two services here and [then] they didn't have them here anymore." Maybe it's because the chapel's rumored to be haunted. "There's supposed to be a murder or hanging out west here," Lester said, though he's a bit skeptical. "I don't know whether there was or whether there wasn't. And there's the Civil War soldier. There's supposed to be two." People have reported seeing Civil War soldiers on

horseback in the cemetery. Others have only heard the horses.

"A week or two weeks before Halloween [2004], I went out in the afternoon with a friend of mine about 3:00 PM," said Jessica Lavicky, a graduate of Northwest Missouri State University. They were checking out the site for a haunted excursion after dark. "It was kind of a muggy, overcast day. We took the dog with us. We walked down to the cemetery and the dog started running back and forth like it was playing with somebody. But it wasn't playing with us." Church bells pealed while they stood between the headstones—too close for nearby Maryville, but not possible for Workman Chapel. The chapel had no bell.

That's when she heard something else out of place. "At the same time we heard horse's hooves in front of us," she said. "We heard it in the front of us and beside us. I thought it was from a field, but there were no horses there." Then they left the cemetery and went inside the church. "We walked in, and it's like this musty feeling, like it's been closed up for years," Jessica said, "which is odd because the doors and windows are gone. In the back, it smelled like somebody lit a match." The musty smell was still there when they came back that night with friends—but that's not all. "We had the dog with us and flashlights and we walked arm in arm," she continued. "The dog was pointing, but there were rabbits enough you couldn't justify it. But when I walked outside the building, I heard hissing. Everyone saw shadows moving and the dog went ape shit. We all went back to the dorm."

Shadows are a common theme at the chapel. Josh LeMar, a former Maryville resident, attended Northwest for three years after graduating from Maryville High School. He had been to the chapel in high school and college. "One night, when we were juniors in high school, we took a bunch of the freshman girls out there, and we had the intentions of scaring them," he said. "We were going to give the code word and all the guys were going to jump in the cars and leave the girls there and come back in about fifteen minutes or so." Somebody gave the code and the guys took off—but not all of them made it. "When we got to a gravel road we realized we left a guy back with the girls," Josh said. "We waited about fifteen to twenty minutes and we pull in and see Bobby, the guy we left behind. He was quite upset." Bobby wanted to know who else the boys left behind. But the boys hadn't left anybody else behind but the girls. "He said, 'That's a bunch of shit. There's somebody out in the graveyard jumping around the headstones.' He'd seen somebody jumping from headstone to headstone and hiding behind them. We loaded everyone up in the cars and got out of there right away." Josh said a friend saw a woman standing at the door of the church one night during a ghost hunt. But the hunters didn't stick around long enough to find out if she was an apparition or a drunken student looking for a ride home. "They got out of there."

Lester doesn't much believe in ghosts, and he doesn't really think anything out of the ordinary goes on at Workman Chapel. "Not unless some college kids honky-tonkin' out here maybe some night," he said. These kids, according to Lester, turn over gravestones—which costs a few hundred dollars to fix. But some young ghost hunters, like Jessica, won't have any part of trouble at Workman Chapel. "When I go back, I don't want to be drinking or disruptive," Jessica said. "I don't want to do anything to disturb the cemetery. I never believed in it before, but now, whoa."

I stayed at the church until a few hours after dark. No lady, no Civil War soldiers, and no bells. But whether I stood inside the building or walked the cemetery grounds, I never felt alone, even though I was. Yeah, Jessica, I'm glad I didn't disturb anything either.

Workman Chapel

Driving directions: From Maryville, take US 71 north to Route FF. Take FF 5.6 miles to County Road 182; turn left on 182. The chapel and cemetery will be on the left.

And watch out for horses. You never know when you might run into a Civil War soldier.

Chapter 20

Hazel Ridge Cemetery
BRUNSWICK

Hazel Ridge Cemetery can't be seen from the rural highway that runs past its entrance, a slice of gravel that sneaks off a nameless blacktop road in Chariton County. I would have missed it if I hadn't been following someone. An old caretaker's house, leaning like a carnival attraction, rots in a grove of saplings at the entrance to Hazel Ridge Cemetery, but I didn't see the shack when I drove in. I'd get there later.

Dark trees leaned over the road as I made my way toward the cemetery, branches turning the long stretch of rocks and dirt into a tunnel. The road slid down and back up steep hills, making me wonder why anyone would have planted a cemetery in such a spot. But the cemetery sits atop a hill, and certain high places have properties that draw things to them—sometimes unexpected things.

Ryan Straub hunts ghosts. I was following him and fellow ghost hunter,

Kurt Ostrom of Chicago, to Hazel Ridge Cemetery. Hazel Ridge's most famous stone belongs to Pettis Perkinson, a pre-Civil War farmer whose slave
B. K. Bruce would later become the first black treasurer of the United States.
Ryan and his ghost hunting group, Tirfirnath (which means "watch and ob-
serve the dead" in Tolkien elvish) have investigated this cemetery before—
numerous times. They're never disappointed with what they experience because they always experience something new. That is because Hazel Ridge
Cemetery is never like they left it.

"The environment seems to change," Ryan said. "I've been to that place
500 times and every time it's different. The whole environment changes.
The trees move. The tombstones move. I know it sounds weird, but … I've
got every section mapped out and they're not the way they were."

Ryan has investigated ghosts since being in a car wreck at age sixteen.
"I was hurt really bad," he recalled. "Then I started seeing things. Even
that night. Spirits. After that I thought, 'What the hell's happening to me?'
I've dedicated my life to it." That includes his education. Ryan is also an
Army interrogator and attends Benedictine University in Chicago, where
he majors in psychology, philosophy, and metaphysics. But he didn't pick
Benedictine for the academics. "It's haunted," he said. "That's the only reason I went to it. It's a Catholic university. There were exorcisms conducted
on the top floor of one building. That's why I went to school here. I heard it
was haunted by demons."

No demons at Hazel Ridge—that the ghost hunters know of—but there
is that moving tombstone thing. "I still don't really know how to explain it,"
said Tirfirnath co-founder Mike Haurcade, a biology major at the University of Missouri-Columbia. "We both drew maps from memory, Ryan and
I, and they both matched. When we got to the cemetery at night, some of
the tombstones didn't match the ones we'd mapped. Some of the trees were
in different places than other times, and some of the larger tombstones
were in different spots. So, unless both of our memories are faulty, something changed."

It has. Kurt has seen it. "I saw a couple of gravestones shift last time,"
Kurt said, standing amidst stones that ranged from the early 1800s to 1987.
And the stones didn't just wiggle. These stones simply went from one place
to another, almost dumping one ghost hunter onto the ground. Dr. Dave
Oester, of the International Ghost Hunters Society, has seen this phenom-
enon in Oklahoma, where a cemetery he investigated suddenly became

a pasture. "What you describe is what we call a dimensional shift," Dave said. "It is where a parallel dimension overlaps into our dimension, transferring the other dimension into our physical dimension, this is why the gravestones shift locations. … This deals with parallel worlds." Ryan may have even seen the gateway to those worlds. "I've come down here before and I've seen a mirage," he said. "I've had a couple of people think there's a vortex, but I wasn't going to walk into it or something stupid like that."

I watched carefully as Kurt and my nine-year-old son, Hayden, walked to a fence on the southern end of the cemetery to look at cattle, just in case a wormhole opened up and sucked them into some bad movie on late-night TV. It didn't. The beasts, placid and fat, would all make fine burgers at some backyard cookout one day. They milled around the pasture eating, as cattle are prone to do. Kurt and Hayden watched them silently through the fence.

The air was cold at Hazel Ridge Cemetery. Hayden and I met the ghost hunters at a convenience store in nearby Brunswick (the pecan capital of Missouri). It was warm for December, maybe 50 degrees, but whether that was the actual temperature or just what the pecans decreed, I wasn't sure. But in the cemetery it was cold enough that I had to don my coat … and I don't like the word "don," so I was in a foul mood. Maybe there was something to the strangeness here.

Cold always accompanies spirits, and there may be a lot of them at Hazel Ridge. Ryan thinks so—he's heard them. Ryan records EVPs and he has picked up some interesting audio in this cemetery, which is far away from houses, highways, and railroad tracks. He pulled a sleek, black recorder out of his jacket pocket and fingered the record button. "I sat it just like that," he showed me, placing the recorder atop a weatherworn, pitted tombstone, "and we walked away from it. The next morning we listened to it and it sounded like chipmunks. I slowed it down and it was a little girl singing 'Ring Around the Rosie.'" The stone where he laid the recorder was near a section of the cemetery that contains children's graves.

Kurt waved at us from the fence line. The cattle had stopped grazing and were looking past Kurt and Hayden and into the cemetery. "Those cows are staring at something," Kurt said. "And it ain't us." Maybe the cattle heard something. Strange noises in Hazel Ridge Cemetery are common. The cattle were quiet—no moos. "I've heard something that sounded like somebody was walking with a metal bucket and it clinked," Ryan said. "My

uncle told me about this place, and he was down here with his girlfriend, and a farmer with a bucket came to the window and he didn't have a face. The guy who used to be the caretaker, his shack burned on the hill. A lot of people think it is him who is doing this."

Yeah, the shack. I looked up at Hayden. He and Kurt were still staring silently at the blank-eyed cattle, hands in their coat pockets, when the cattle, like a flock of birds suddenly changing direction for no apparent reason, turned and ran. "It was like they saw something behind us and just got spooked," Kurt said. Maybe so.

We walked down the hill from the cemetery back toward the road, the overhanging trees dimming the light. The cold backed away too—probably because we had walked off the hill, but I didn't want to easily brush off the possibility that the cemetery was just weird. At the bottom of the hill, Hayden laughed at a T-shirt hanging off a tree limb stretching over a stream that was an illegal dumping ground for old water heaters and La-Z-Boys. We climbed over another hill that led toward the highway.

Ryan had seen something at the base of this hill, right where we were walking—something that spooked him. "Mike and I, we were leaving one day," he began. "As we were leaving, we were in the middle of the hills and we saw a very large dog in the road. It stood up on its hind legs and left the road." Its appearance (and sudden disappearance) is the only paranormal event that has ever really disturbed him. "That bothered me a little bit. The only thing I could think of was the mythical beast the werewolf." Uh, okay. I guess it was a good thing it was still daylight and the full moon was days ahead of us. That is, of course, if you are thinking of the Hollywood model of lycanthropy and not the French model from 1682, which is the last time France was cool. Back then, werewolves could come out anytime they wanted.

Near the top of the next hill at the blacktop road, we stepped off the gravel and fought our way through briars and saplings until we reached the caretaker's shack. It had been abandoned for years. The building leaned to the south, giving its doors and windows the look of something a kid put together. "Every time I've gone in there, it's been harder and harder each time," Ryan said. It's like the building didn't want to be bothered. "I've been here 500 times, and that's no exaggeration, and I'd never seen it."

As we walked closer to the structure, pieces of ancient farm equipment that could grace a museum display sat rusting among trees that had grown too close to the house. A sink, a chair, and a table, were strewn across what was once a yard. Ryan stepped through the fun house doorway and into the shack. Two old crank washers sat on the rotting floor of the house, along with a few odds and ends of furniture that never made it out.

"It feels weird in this place," Ryan said. "It feels like there's someone else here with us. Like we're not supposed to be here. It's hard to breathe." I didn't feel uncomfortable there, but I noticed the sound had died. I could hear us, but nothing else. No wind, no distant traffic, no birds. Nothing. We didn't stay much longer. Was the shack haunted? "Anyplace can be haunted," Ryan said as we pushed back through the brush. "If you see a ghost in your house, it doesn't mean it's haunted. Spirits travel. Schools are good. Old hospitals. Cemeteries. It just depends on the type of spirit you're looking for."

Kurt's cell phone rang when we stepped back onto the road. He tried to answer it, but the signal died. "This place doesn't like cell phones," he explained. But 'this place' didn't like a lot of things. "My truck didn't start at times," Ryan said. "Flashlights will die up here quick too." Kurt pocketed his cell phone, giving up on a signal. "A lot of things die up here," he said.

As we approached Hazel Ridge, where a great wooden cross loomed like a vulture at the entrance to the cemetery, the temperature dropped again. Sure, it was probably the elevation, but still, it was damned cold—ghost cold. Yeah, could be. The cross and the end of the gravel marked a gateway into the graveyard, and gateways let things in … and out. "A threshold is a gateway to everything," Ryan said. "A doorway's a threshold. Anything where two planes meet, where the lines blur, there's more of a chance spirits will come through."

Ryan, Mike, and Kurt have all seen things in Hazel Ridge Cemetery they couldn't explain. "The first time [I stayed the night] I had a pup tent," Ryan told me. "I had my pup tent spread out and turned around to get a hammer, and when I turned around, the tent was folded up and in the box."

Lights, noises, and other paranormal phenomenon throughout the world have commonly been explained away as tricks of light and shadow, atmospheric disturbances, and gasses escaping from the ground. Ryan and Mike explore these avenues before pinning the supernatural tag on an experience. "We both look at physics," Ryan said. "We try to recreate a piece of evidence over and over until we prove it or disprove it. [But] I don't think gasses can put a tent back in a box."

And ghosts have made themselves visible at Hazel Ridge. Kurt once saw a man in early 1800s clothing standing in the cemetery. "In this back corner," Kurt said, standing in the southwestern part of the cemetery. "I saw a large shadow figure. I don't know what it was, but it wasn't pretty." Mike saw something similar too. Two groups of ghost hunters were walking around the cemetery one evening when Mike saw a man peering at him from behind a tree. "I shined my flashlight at it and it froze," he said.

Ryan was in the second group, and could see Mike's group and the back of the tree, but he didn't see the man. "I saw someone standing behind the tree, and I could see their head and shoulder, and I thought it was part of the other group," Mike continued. He turned toward the other members of his group and they were looking past him at whoever—whatever—it was. "It wasn't any of us. At that point I turned back toward the tree and couldn't see anything at all." "It would have been in our line of sight too," Ryan added. "I've seen and heard some other odd things," Mike said. "But [the dark figure] I can't dispel."

I didn't hear anything odd at Hazel Ridge, but it felt funny. Hayden just climbed the big tombstones from the 1880s and occasionally waved at me. Nothing feels funny to a nine-year-old unless you try to make them eat vegetables. Things just seemed dampened at Hazel Ridge Cemetery— duller, grayer. There's something strange in that place. I don't know what it is, but Ryan and his group are trying to find out.

"The reason why I started putting this group together is to show people there's more," Ryan said. "The group focuses on finding answers. There have been things I haven't been able to prove. I'm just out there to see if I can."

Hazel Ridge Cemetery

Driving directions: From U.S. 24 in Brunswick, turn north on Scott Street, which becomes N. Keyte Street. Turn right on Cass, then left on Herring. Continue north on Herring for 4 miles (road becomes gravel), then turn right onto an unnamed gravel road.

Tirfirnath e-mail: melinko4@hotmail.com.

Chapter 21

Peace Church Cemetery
JOPLIN

Peace Church Cemetery is lonely at dusk. Tall grass and weeds hide the older headstones, some of which date back to the early 1800s. According to local historians at the Joplin Public Library, no one regularly cares for the cemetery nowadays—the Boy Scouts used to trim the lawn, but not anymore. Once a year, the county burns off the weeds, leaving uneven clumps of tombstones rising from the ash, like jagged stumps in a long-dead forest. A few people visit to place flowers on the graves of parents or grandparents. But the cemetery's most famous guest is nowhere to be found. A serial killer who was buried under the anonymity of night lies in an unmarked grave at Peace Church Cemetery, hidden from the curious and, at one time, vengeful.

Joplin is the hometown of poet, novelist, and playwright Langston Hughes, Missouri Southern State University, and NASCAR driver Jamie McMurray. Just outside of the town limits, a dirt road, grass growing between the tire tracks, winds into the cemetery. The air was thick, as Missouri summers tend to be, and the cemetery was quiet, disturbed only by a pickup making its way over the hill that hugs the cemetery.

Billy Cook is buried in this quiet place. "Badman Bill Cook, mad dog killer of six persons" headlines a 1952 *Joplin Globe* article. He killed a family of five

and a random motorist during a 1951 cross-country murder spree. His story was the subject of the 1953 movie *The Hitchhiker* and is referenced in the 1971 Doors song, "Riders on the Storm." Some say they have seen the killer walking the grounds at night, a black shadow weaving through the trees. Others have reported strange lights. Still others have heard voices. I didn't know if I would find Cook here tonight, but I was pretty sure I didn't want to.

Peace Church was built on the homestead of Peter R. Johnson in the early 1850s, according to a May 6, 1956, article in the *Joplin Globe*. Johnson raised sixteen children on that land, before it was turned into a place for salvation. One of the earliest settlers in Jasper County, a man named Thacker Vivion, was the first person to preach at Peace Church. But peace didn't last long in the area, and the Civil War was soon upon Missouri. "Early Joplin settlers thought there was a 'haint,' as they called it, in that area," said Steve Cottrell, a Civil War historian from nearby Carthage. "Kind of a hillbilly-type term for a haunted place. What it stems from is from the Civil War. That site was a site of a horrendous attack." Union troops (the First Kansas Colored Infantry) stopped for food at the Rader Farm, which was close to the present-day cemetery. The locals, including the Rader family, were Southern sympathizers. "The [soldiers] were gathering corn for their camp in the Baxter Springs area when they were surprised and were decimated [by Confederate troops]," Cottrell said. "The survivors made their way across the state line that night to their camp." The next day a detachment of their fellow soldiers rode back to Joplin, stacked the remains of their comrades in the Rader house, and burned it down. Because of local superstition, the land remained empty for the next twenty years.

"There was just a rumor for years that the place was haunted," Cottrell said. "But in the 1880s, a family by the name of Snapp, they just snubbed local superstition, built a nice, two-story home on the site and everything was fine, as far as we know." But in 1937, the Snapp home was burned to the ground by a mysterious fire. "Like the Rader home before it," Cottrell explained, "the Snapp home burnt to the ground. That's where the legend comes from."

Confederate soldiers buried in unmarked graves in Peace Church Cemetery started the stories, but the burial of twenty-three-year-old Billy Cook in 1952 only made the legend of the haint stronger. The cinder-block entrance to the cemetery was broken, and busted beer bottles littered the ground. The edges of thick trees surrounding the grounds were starting to grow ominous in the quickly fading daylight. From that spot I could see the entire cemetery, but there was no point in looking there for Cook's grave. "His dad is buried there," said Amanda Powell, reference clerk at the Joplin Public Library. The Cook family has a plot in the cemetery, but Billy isn't in it. He's buried somewhere outside the boundaries of the cemetery. So if I were going to find Billy, it sure wasn't going to be below ground.

Billy Cook was born the fifth of eight children on December 23, 1928, in a windowless, one-room shack outside Joplin. His father abandoned the family when Billy was five years old, and his mother died a year later. Cook grew up in relatives' homes, foster homes, reform school, and later, the state penitentiary for various assaults and robberies. Cook had been born with a growth over his right eye and, though the growth was later removed, his right eyelid always sagged, earning him nicknames, and one more excuse to be angry. On December 31, 1950, the Mosser family—Carl, Thelma, and their three children—of Atwood, Illinois, were on vacation when a hitchhiking Cook kidnapped the family and forced them to drive throughout the Southwest before taking them to Joplin and shooting them all. "He killed the dog too," Amanda said.

After dumping the Mosser family down an abandoned mine shaft, Cook wandered back across the Southwest to Blythe, California, where he kidnapped a sheriff's deputy and confessed to seven murders, though no one has ever determined if he had actually committed two of the other murders. Cook dropped the deputy on the side of the road and later murdered a traveling salesman from Seattle just to take his car. Police finally arrested Cook 600 miles south of the Mexican border. In 1951, Cook was sentenced to 300 years in prison for the murders of the Mosser family. According to

a *Time* magazine article, the prosecutor left the courtroom shouting, "the goddamdest travesty on justice, ever." Cook was later sentenced to death for the murder of the salesman. He was put to death in the gas chamber at the San Quentin penitentiary. *Life* magazine (January 29, 1951) ran the story of the "mad dog murderer," featuring a picture of his fingers tattooed with the words 'Hard Luck.' "The tattooed legend that he had stenciled on fingers in reformatory tells Cook's self-pitying philosophy," the *Life* caption read. "Girls never liked him; he won respect of males only with his fists."

After 12,000 curious onlookers viewed Cook's body in Comanche, Oklahoma, Cook was brought to Joplin. "Badman Bill Cook is buried at night in Peace Cemetery," read the headline of a 1952 *Joplin Globe* story by reporter Gerald Wallace. The ten-minute graveside service was offici-ated by the Rev. Dow Booe of nearby Galena. "Brief service held at night with aid of flashlights and lanterns before about fifteen persons;" "Funeral cortege, consisting of four cars and hearse, moves to burial place over back roads," the sub-headlines read. "Just as the graveside rites ended," Wallace wrote, "the cry of a small child could be heard in the chill of the night air."

Local paranormal groups have investigated Peace Church Cemetery and, though they haven't turned up Billy Cook, they have measured magnetic fluc-tuations in the cemetery, according to a 2004 article in the *Joplin Globe*. There was an odd stillness to the cemetery as I wandered through the grounds on my way back to the car. On the one hand, I was dissatisfied, but I was happy I hadn't conjured up Billy Cook. Whether that stillness could be attributed to the thick growth of trees and the hills that isolated this spot, or to the painful, bloody history of the land, I didn't know. All I knew was nightfall was close and I didn't want to be there anymore. "I've been out there," Amanda said. "It's kind of creepy." Yes, I thought, my ghost hunting trip came up empty, but Amanda was right—Peace Church Cemetery is awfully creepy.

Peace Church Cemetery

Driving directions: From Joplin, travel west on Seventh Street; turn right on Shiffendecker Road just past the Shiffend-ecker Golf Course and continue north through a Y-intersection at the city limits of Joplin. Continue to a T-intersection and turn left. The cemetery will be on the right.

Chapter 22

Glore Psychiatric Museum
ST. JOSEPH

A sign reading "Warning—Missouri Department of Corrections Property—No Trespassing—Violators Subject to Prosecution" is planted outside a fenced yard at the Western Reception Diagnostic and Correctional Center in St. Joseph. The 127-year-old building sits behind the St. Joseph Museum offices and is home to 595 offenders in substance abuse treatment programs. But in November 1874, the building opened as State Lunatic Asylum No. 2, a home to the mentally ill, epileptics, drunkards, and the unwanted, many of whom are buried on the grounds. The building burned, and after it was rebuilt in 1879, it housed the state psychiatric hospital until 1997 when the Missouri Department of Corrections took over the facility and moved the mental hospital and Glore Psychiatric Museum into a building next door. But both buildings have seen the insane and the dead, some of whom are still there—and have been for a long time.

St. Joseph of the 1870s was a busy place. Many people were seeking their fortunes west, and the state figured a busy town was a good spot for

an asylum. "I think they chose St. Joseph because of the migration," said Scott Clark, former St. Joseph Museum director. "St. Joseph was such a growing town. Because of the people traveling west, it was very easy to drop somebody off here. If Uncle Fred was acting strangely, just drop him off with the clothes you want him buried in because he's probably not going to leave. That's what [they'd] tell them, just pretend like they were dead."

Those who died in the asylum, some killed by fellow inmates, were buried in a graveyard on the property. And for people without names or families to claim them, the method of marking the graves was clear. "There's a patient cemetery with 2,000 graves not named, just numbered," Scott explained. "I think that's why some of the spirits wander the halls." George Glore, former director for whom the psychiatric museum is named, worked forty-one years for the Department of Mental Health, and he's familiar with strange happenings in the former asylum. "The patients and staff in that building were continually talking about seeing a lady in a flowing gown in the museum at night," he said.

Who was the spectral lady? No one knows. But with 2,000 graves on the property, none of them named, she could have been anybody, and she could be more than 130 years old. The first deaths at the asylum were in December 1874. "Two people died," Scott told me. "The weather had to have been so bad and the guys just dug one hole. The No. 2 hole was buried in January that next year." By the 1940s, there were about 3,000 beds in the mental hospital that held people with disorders understood today. "There was Alzheimer's, alcoholism, epilepsy, just a lot of people people didn't want to deal with," Scott said. A lot of these patients died at the hospital with no family and no identity. The last burial on record was in 1949. "There are a lot of people who can't rest in peace because their families just discarded them," he said. "We have names to some, but there's just a lot of troubled souls down in the graveyard."

Some of those troubled souls may have kept Myrna Hopkins company. Myrna worked as an administrative assistant for George and later Scott before retiring in 2002. She and other staff members at the museum used to see things, but just in the periphery. "We used to feel like you could almost see somebody go by," she said. "You'd be sitting there typing, and you'd just kinda see something, and then you'd go on. It was mainly just a feeling like somebody was always there with you. You weren't ever alone. I worked there thirty-five years so I kinda got used to it. When you're young, you're young and dumb, but when you're older, you just learn to live with it." A patient at the psychiatric hospital learned to live with the ghosts. "We used to have a patient in the center building who wrote poetry and stories about the ghosts in the building," George said. "Everybody pooh-poohed that, but she swore they were real. Certainly she was mentally ill or she wouldn't have been there, but she was pretty lucid."

Some experts explain hauntings as spirits who stay on earth to finish unfinished business or spirits who stay simply because they don't know they're dead. A hundred years ago, mental illness was not well understood and patients at mental institutions received little or no treatment, and through the 1950s, the psychiatric field didn't do much to alleviate shock or trauma to institutionalized patients—hardly a situation that would encourage the departed to rest in peace. "When I started, there was neglect, patient abuse, overcrowding. And really some undesirable situations patients found themselves in," George began. "There have been some tremendous changes with the care of the patients, and tremendous changes toward the attitude for the mentally ill." But whatever time period, or whatever mental state the spirits were in when they passed, they sure spook some people. "We had a music therapist who was later relocated to that floor where the museum used to be," he continued. "He would hear noises. He wouldn't work there alone."

George has his own feelings about the building, but he's not ready to admit they were ghostly visits. "I used to go out and work evenings in the museum," he said, "and I'd get spooked. But I'd just assume it was the building settling. I did have two or three instances in the evening where the hair would kind of stand up on the back of my neck. But after you work in a state mental hospital for a while, you just learn to accept a lot of things."

Steve Cline, associate superintendent of the Western Reception Diagnostic and Correctional Center, hasn't accepted the ghosts of the old building. He hasn't had to. "We've been in the buildings here for quite some time now," Steve said. "And I personally cannot relate or recall any observations or complaints from staff or offenders. In a correctional setting, if we'd had any trouble, I'd be the first one to hear about it."

I couldn't get into the correctional facility—it wasn't visiting day. Even if it were, the visiting public wouldn't have been allowed to roam places where patients have screamed and suffered throughout the decades. That is where I wanted to go—the old hallways and the patient rooms. But I went to the current location of the Glore Psychiatric Museum, which is within walking (and maybe tunneling) distance from the correctional facility, and it has enough stories of its own.

"We moved out and moved into the new facility in 1997," George told me. "I said 'we'—the hospital did. I started the museum in 1966, and it opened in 1967 officially. Then we kept adding to it over the years." George worked as the museum's curator "without that title until 1983." He retired as curator in 1996. The current home of the Glore Psychiatric Museum is in a building constructed in 1969. The black and gold "Fallout Shelter" sign seemed a little out of place with the early 1900s grinding stone and other turn of the century farm equipment stored in the halls of the museum basement, but it was oddly comforting. Wooden peg legs are on display there, too, along with a jukebox, a couple of classic cars, and the morgue. The morgue/autopsy room has been in the same spot since the building was constructed—and is still operational. The temperature inside the four-body stainless steel refrigeration units is kept at about 40 degrees. The morgue used to hold the bodies of dead mental patients until family members made funeral home arrangements, and was used "for autopsies of deaths that involved foul play," Scott said.

Murder, whether it resembles an Alfred Hitchcock movie or *The Bride of Chucky*, is all the same. And maybe some spirits, restless from a dirty deed that was scientifically pinpointed in the hospital basement, are still wandering around. "People would not go downstairs at night," Scott said. "We had a working morgue there. The hair would raise up on the back of your neck. There were a couple of times that I left the building in a hurry because of some of the experiences. The one case I really, really got spooked. I had broken my leg in a car wreck and was trying to hobble with a cane," he said. "It was a holiday, so the building was locked up. I was alone there. As I came out of my office, my cane caught on something. I looked down to see what I had stumbled over. When I looked up, something passed [between] me and the stairs. The doors were closed."

And it's not just museum staff or psychiatric patients who have experienced otherworldly phenomena at the museum. Guests are not immune to the dead. "I've had visitors come in and tell me they've had an overwhelming experience with the sprits," Scott said. "This gal came in, a psychic, she says, 'Are there spirits in there?' And I said, 'Sure'. ... She said she was led in the building and felt like she was hit in the gut because of the activity there.

I'm not saying I was a firm believer before I worked there, but I feel there are poltergeists or spirits in the building."

Standing alone in the basement of the Glore Psychiatric Museum, snapping pictures of stainless steel body fridges, I felt a little creeped out. Whether my unease came from the stories, the spirits, or the more horrific displays of the history of mental health in America, I didn't know. All I knew was that the hospital and museum corridors were good places to wander if you were a ghost. Or if you just wanted to find a ghost.

Glore Psychiatric Museum

3406 Frederick Avenue, St. Joseph, MO 64508

Phone: 816/232-8471 (toll free 800/530-8866)
Website: www.stjosephmuseum.org
Hours: 10 AM–5 PM Monday through Saturday; 1–5 PM Sunday.
Admission: adults $3; students (7–18) $1; children 6 and under free

Returning to Their Old Haunts

Over the years, the Show-Me State has hosted many famous visitors: presidents, statesmen, gangsters, military leaders, athletes, entertainers, and ruffians. Some came on official business, others for tourism. Many visitors have left their mark in guest books, and many famous or influential people have left their marks in more significant ways. Most leave when their stay has ended, but some, like Jesse and Frank James, liked their stay so much they don't want to leave—even when their bodies lie dead in the cold, wet ground.

Mark Twain Cave
H-ANNIB-AL

I stepped across the dark, chilly entrance to Hannibal's Mark Twain Cave and swung the metal gate closed behind me with a clank, shutting out anyone who thought of getting in without paying. I gained the right to shut the door simply because I was the last person in my tour group ... and the seventeen-year-old tour guide said I could. I latched the gate and moved quickly in the darkness to catch up with the group, smiling because I knew something the gray-haired man with his grandkids, the tourists from Wisconsin, and the young couple from Illinois didn't. I knew the cave was haunted.

The town of Hannibal is dominated by businesses whose names are drawn from Mark Twain's stories—Becky Thatcher's Café, Huck Finn Shopping Center, Injun Joe Campground, Twainland Express Depot, Hotel Clemens, and Sawyer's Creek. But I was visiting a place that Mark Twain

had actually spent a considerable amount of time, and which is now named for him. A young Samuel Clemens would often hike three miles to visit this cave, which he would eventually introduce to the world in *The Adventures of Tom Sawyer*. "I seemed to tire of most everything I did," Twain wrote in his autobiography. "But I never tired of exploring the cave." The metal gate I had pulled shut to block the great, stone-worked entrance to the cave didn't exist in Twain's time. The entrance didn't either. Townsfolk blasted the entrance in 1890 to accommodate the growing crowds of people who had visited the cave since the 1876 publication of *Tom Sawyer*. About 60,000 to 70,000 people still visit Mark Twain Cave each year. "Sometimes more," said Susie Shelton, general manager. "I'm planning on more this year."

The cave formed about 100 million years ago as water from a great inland sea that covered the Midwest washed away softer earth and rock, leav-

ing miles of passages Twain described (in *Tom Sawyer*) as "a labyrinth of crooked aisles that ran into each other and out again and led nowhere. It was said that one might wander days and nights together through its intricate tangle of rifts and chasms and never find the end of the cave." The cave was discovered in 1819 by local farmer and hunter Jack Sims, "when he was out hunting and his dogs chased a panther into this little opening," Susie said. "He covered up the opening and when he came back the next day, nothing had changed. He sent the dogs in and the dogs got lost. So he went in and discovered what is now called Mark Twain Cave."

The six and a half mile cave is 52 degrees all year long. A big round thermometer in the cave keeps you aware of that. Because of the temperature, the cave has hosted town meetings and six weddings; it also served as a bomb shelter during the Cold War. As we walked deeper into the cave, the kids in the group soon gripped their sides complaining about the temperature that had dropped at least 35 degrees from aboveground.

The cave has been, and still is, privately owned. But one owner during Twain's time, Dr. Joseph Nash McDowell, a surgeon from St. Louis who founded the Missouri Medical College, made the cave creepy. "He was trying to petrify a human body," Susie said. "His own daughter died of pneumonia at fourteen. He took a copper cylinder lined with glass. He filled it with an alcohol mixture, put in his daughter, and hung it from a ceiling in a cave room. The kids would go back in there and tell ghost stories."

One of those kids, according to Susie, was a young Samuel Clemens. "The top of the cylinder was removable," Twain wrote in *Life on the Mississippi*. "And it was said to be a common thing for the baser order of tourists to drag the dead face into view and examine it and comment upon it." After enough children ran home crying to momma, parents began to complain to the doctor. "Two years later, after protest from Hannibal, Dr. McDowell removed her from the cave," Susie said. "She was well preserved, but was not petrified." Although the body of Dr. McDowell's daughter is in the family mausoleum in St. Louis, her restless spirit may still be in the cave where she hung for two years, a science project for her father and a plaything for tourists. "I've had guides say they've seen somebody," Susie said. "I've been in and out of there fifteen years and have never seen or felt anything. I grew up in a house with ghosts and I think I'd feel something. I do understand ghosts."

Tom Rickey was a tour guide at the cave in the late 1990s when he saw something that still makes him shudder. "I got a cold chill," he said. "I got them now thinking about it. I wasn't scared, surprisingly enough. I got a chill over me, and I turned around and she was there." Tom was exploring the cave alone when he saw a girl who shouldn't have been there. "I was back through there walking through the cave and I happened to look back in McDowell's room … and I saw her standing there as plain as day," Tom said. "She had long dark hair. Very, very pretty. She was only there for an instant." The girl wore a long, "evening gown-type" dress with a cape, Tom said—a dress like girls wore in the mid-1800s.

"I tried to speak to her, because I thought she was somebody lost," Tom explained. "But I started to and she left." He followed her into the cave room and found out that, no, she wasn't a tourist. "She walked off. She didn't fade away, but there wasn't nowhere to walk. She went through the wall. She just walked off and she wasn't there anymore. I knew who she was." Tom said at that time a picture of the girl hung on the ceiling in that room. "When I looked on the ceiling, I could see her perfect," he said. "I recognized who she was. When I saw her, there was no disbelief, no sadness on her facial expression. She had a smile on her face. That, I will never forget. I'm not sure what the smile means because he froze her back there. He did the experiment on her. I don't know why she'd smile, but she did." Tom hurried out of the cave and told the other guides about the girl. "They believed me because they've had experiences in there before."

Susie said Tom's experience isn't isolated. "There have been stories of people seeing a little girl in there, so it's possible," she said. "I've had a few tour guides who've said they've felt something. Some guides don't like to go in there by themselves."

Tour guide Jamie Buckman, a Hannibal High School student, led my group past the entrance to the room where the doctor conducted his experiment, but it is off limits to tourists. That didn't stop Jamie from flicking the already dim lights as he told the doctor's story. Although the story of McDowell's daughter is the most gruesome, her body hasn't been the only one to lie in Mark Twain Cave. Three Civil War draft dodgers were found dead there. Names written and carved into the limestone decorate the walls of certain sections of the cave. Leaving an autograph in the cave was a tradition from 1820 to the moment it became a registered national landmark in 1972. The most famous of those is a signature Jesse James wrote in pencil. Handwriting experts have confirmed the signature is James'.

"There are more than 6,000 caves in [the] state," Jamie told the group. "There are twenty-two show caves. Seventeen claim Jesse James stayed in [their] cave. We're the only one with proof." Of the eighteen spots along the tour, with names like Injun Joe's Canoe and Treasure Room, Aladdin's Palace is the only room in the cave Twain named himself, Jamie said. He named it after his favorite book, *Arabian Nights*. Although Jamie's never experienced anything ill in Mark Twain Cave, he has in nearby Cameron Cave.

"One part of the cave is right underneath an old Irish cemetery that

dates back to the 1830s or 1840s," Jamie said. "When I go in there sometimes I can't tell if it's the shadow of a light, but it's something that swishes
by." Nothing swished by on my trip through Mark Twain Cave—not even
one of the cave's small population of thumb-sized bats—but that doesn't
mean no one's home. "Things are out there," Tom said. "Oh, yeah."

Mark Twain Cave

300 Cave Hollow Road, Hannibal, MO 63401

Phone: 573/221-1656 (toll free 800/527-0304)
Website: www.marktwaincave.com
Hours: Summer 9 AM-8 PM; Winter 9 AM-4 PM;
Spring and Fall 9 AM-6 PM; closed Christmas and
Thanksgiving
Admission: 13 and over $14; children 5-12 $7

Chapter 24

The Elms Resort and Spa

EXCELSIOR SPRINGS

The Elms Resort Hotel and Spa sits at the bottom of a hill next to a mean-dering tributary named Fishing River that snakes its way through the town of Excelsior Springs on its way to the Big Muddy. But the brown, swirling water of Fishing River isn't why people have come to The Elms Resort and Spa for a more than a century. The healing powers of the area's mineral springs that gave the town its name have attracted people to The Elms Ho-tel since the turn of the twentieth century. The Elms has hosted mobsters, professional athletes, and at least two American presidents. It still hosts some guests who just never left.

On the afternoon I arrived at The Elms, an oddly uniform space-alien-gray sheet of clouds stretched to the horizons. The hotel looked much as it did in pictures from the 1910s kept in the Excelsior Springs Historical Mu-seum. To maintain the ambiance, various owners of The Elms over the years have worked to keep the building looking that way—like you are stepping

back into 1912. I walked into the hotel without asking for directions because I knew exactly where I was going. I had worked as a bartender at the hotel in 1989 and was familiar with the layout. I wasn't familiar with the ghosts of The Elms from my barman stint—I wasn't there long enough to hear many stories—but I remember that going into the dark, quiet back rooms of the hotel to restock the bar scared the heck out of me. And it should have. A hotel has existed on the grounds since 1888, but hotels have burned down twice with a few fatalities, and I saw a golfer die at the front door one evening after coming in from thirty-six holes, so there is certainly a good chance a restless spirit or two have been chained to The Elms.

An antique boiler lid is on display downstairs at the hotel. The large round lid was part of a boiler system that used steam to heat the big hotel in the early days. It also survived the fire that rushed through the hotel during a masquerade ball in 1910, sending guests running out into the night. "They said there were no fatalities, but they were just talking about guests," said John Mormino, front office manager at The Elms from its last restoration in 1998 until 2004. "They didn't take into consideration the coal shovelers." Noises ring out in the ground floor of the hotel almost every night—the time the men died. "You can hear them banging," Mormino said. "Banging on pipes still in the walls. But the pipes are not hooked up to the heating system." The banging has been heard by employees and hotel guests alike. And if guests ask about it. ... "Honestly?" Mormino said,"we act surprised and offer to move them."

But there are other events that occur at The Elms, events employees there can't explain. A shaking chandelier in the grand ballroom, the hum of a phantom vacuum sweeper a former manager chased around an entire floor, encounters at the hotel's European lap pool reportedly by the spirit of a bootlegger who died during Prohibition, and a presence in room 505 that bumped a hotel employee, then locked him inside. Room 505 didn't present any resistance as I entered, looked around, and snapped a few pictures. Camille Morales, sales and marketing manager for The Elms, said the employee had finally gotten out of the room, but wouldn't go back in. I grabbed the door handle to leave 505 and it was ... well, it wasn't locked. Maybe the ghost liked me, or maybe it wasn't there. But other spirits may inhabit the hotel, which has been an overnight home to presidents Franklin Delano Roosevelt and Harry S. Truman, fighter Jack Dempsey, the Chicago Bears, and gangster Al Capone. I walked into the hallway from room 505 and down to room 501.

The ghost might be in that room. It has been there before.

"One night, after the hotel opened, our CEO, who stayed in 501, went home to Connecticut," said Bari Allen, a ten-year employee of The Elms. "About two in the morning, a fire alarm went off and a phone at the front desk rang while we were waiting for the fire department. There was no one there. It rang again. There was no one there. It rang every two minutes." The call was coming from room 501. "I went up and no one was there," he said. When Allen returned, the receptionist told him the telephone rang again while he was in room 501—even after Allen had unplugged the phone. "Eventually," Allen said, "it stopped."

Another ghost at the hotel is reportedly the spirit of a maid wearing a 1920s-style uniform. Members of the housekeeping staff who have seen her have said she looks like she is supervising them. According to local legend, the spirit is a grieving mother searching for a lost child who drowned in the hotel pool. But the ghosts of The Elms aren't confined to the hotel itself. Guests and employees have seen activity out by the gazebo. One winter evening, when Mormino was working the night shift, he got a call he felt was, well, odd. "Guests said there was a guy in a white T-shirt and pants at the gazebo," Mormino told me. "He was pacing back and forth. He seemed angry." Mormino walked out to the gazebo, through the freshly fallen snow.

"There was snow everywhere," he said. But the gazebo was empty. No angry guy in a T-shirt, and no footprints in the new snow. Mormino said other guests have reported spotting a man at the gazebo at odd times, but the man who disappeared leaving no tracks in the snow convinced him something otherworldly was happening at The Elms.

And what does hotel management think of their permanent guests? "The stance we've taken in the past is that we're not haunted," Morales said. "And if we are haunted, they're nice."

THe Elms Resort and Spa

401 Regent Street, Excelsior Springs, MO 64024

Phone: 816/630-5500 (toll free 800/843-3567)
Website: www.elmsresort.com

Chapter 25

Jesse James Farm
KEARNEY

Historian Thomas Holloway stood on the wooden deck outside the Jesse James Farm Museum smoking Pall Malls, the edges of his white mustache yellowed by tobacco. Thomas had an affinity for the James family—Frank and his wife, Annie, especially—and worked as a historical interpreter at the farm east of Kearney from 2002 to 2005, studying what he could about the couple and the family made famous by the gun. "I have been very fascinated of the real Jesse James," Thomas said, smoke rolling from his mouth. "Not the stories of myth and fables. He was even more bloodthirsty than the books say he is."

The most famous outlaw in American history, Jesse Woodson James, was born on the farm September 5, 1847, the son of the Reverend Robert and Zerelda James. His older brother Frank, a Civil War soldier, train robber, and celebrity, was born in Kentucky, but died on the farm grounds. But then again, a lot of people died on the 205 acres the James boys' father bought from

Liberty businessman Robert Gilmer in 1845. The James boys were trouble, but their lives as thieves, killers, and outlaws began with the War Between the States. "Jesse was caught up in the Civil War," Thomas said. "He hated it when Frank went to war and he didn't [because he was underage]. Jesse James was a cold-blooded murderer. He was not a Robin Hood."

Thomas' jeans and a blue jean jacket did little against the cold wind of the December day when I visited the James Farm. He kept his hands in his pockets, unless he was lighting another cigarette. Thomas told me the story of Frank and Annie as we left the museum and walked down the winding dirt trail toward the house. They adored each other, he said, even though she didn't approve of his brother Jesse. The trail brushed a creek where the James boys swam and played when they were children. Before stepping through a break in the fence that surrounded the farmhouse, Thomas dropped the spent cigarette to the ground and crushed it with his shoe. Smoking wasn't allowed around history. And at the James Farm, sometimes you don't visit history, history visits you.

"It was spring a year or so before I left here," Thomas recalled, motioning me to the front steps of the home. "Early spring. No guests at the time. Early in the spring, early in the day. I was relaxing, the sun was shining." From the porch steps where Thomas had been that day, awaiting visitors, I watched him back about 20 feet away to the spot where he had seen his first visitor of the morning—a woman who had died in 1944. "I sort of dozed just a little bit and I suddenly had the feeling I wasn't alone," he said. "I sort of came to and standing out in front of me was the figure of a woman. A rather small woman wearing a straight black dress of the period. It occurred to me at the time, 'My God, that's Annie,' then. . . ." Thomas snapped his fingers. "She was gone, but it was so clear." From that distance at that time of day, it would have been tough to mistake anything for a woman in black dress without a heck of a special effects budget. Thomas had been studying Frank and Annie James, and was sure the apparition was her. After Jesse's death, Annie didn't like the attention the farm garnered, according to Thomas. Frank would greet visitors by the front gate and give tours of the farm. Annie hated it, so she stayed at the farmhouse, where Thomas and I stood. "Whether it was my imagination or if it really happened, it was as real as you standing there," Thomas said. "I recognized the person. I knew who it had to be. The size, the black dress she wore."

The interior of the James home was dark that day. A bed where Frank had slept still sits in the front room, along with pieces of period furniture, a number of them donated by the James descendents. The house has seen a lot of history, not much of it good. The James gang planned robberies there, and on January 26, 1875, the Pinkerton Detective Agency attempted a raid on the house, tossing incendiary devices in through the window. The house didn't burn, but the James boys' mother, Zerelda, lost her right arm to the elbow and their eight-year-old stepbrother, Archie Samuel, was mortally wounded.

Frank died at the house in 1915 and Jesse remained buried there until his remains were exhumed and moved to Mount Olivet Cemetery in Kearney. Jesse's wife, Zerelda, who was also his first cousin, is buried there too. Yes, Jesse's mother and wife were both named Zerelda. Any guess as to what side of the family his wife was from?

Psychic Joyce Morgan of Kingston, Missouri, says the family still visits the house when they want to; she has seen them. "As far as the house being haunted, yes," she said. "The James house is haunted." Joyce, a member of the Missouri-based Miller Paranormal Research group, has been able to see and speak with the dead all her life. She has used her gift to help police find missing persons, and two of her cases have been featured on Court TV. "I close my eyes and see a dead body and see where it's at," she said. "Or just close my eyes and know who was in the room at the time. It's with the mind's eye, just like on a television." And, just like that, she has seen the James family at the farm. "I've definitely seen them and I've felt them," she told me. "I saw Frank standing on the porch one time and, my, he was tall. I saw him when he was gray haired, and I saw Annie, and she was so beautiful. I saw Zerelda walk around the corner of the house one time. I have seen Archie running in the yard."

She also witnessed a scene with the James boys' mother seldom discussed by historians. "My feelings are that there was a Pinkerton man that had rode in; I could see him," she said. "He came into the kitchen and sat down. She invited him in. She knew he was there looking for the boys and shot him. The boys came home and buried him, and he's buried on the farm."

"They talk to me," she said of the ghosts. "They just tell me things." Some of those messages are about murders, train robberies, and the war, but other messages are more personal than is rarely discussed about the James family. "Jesse loved Zerelda. Always had," Joyce said. "And Frank loved Annie so very much. He just adored her. Just absolutely adored her. Zerelda [the

mother], all of the history books say that she was strong willed, and she was, and the feelings I get from her, she was strong willed, but she had to be a strong, strong, strong woman to survive all she survived all those years."

Others without Joyce's gift have seen things at the farm too. Some experiences they can explain away and others they can't. Linda Brookshier, who worked as a historical interpreter at the farm for a couple of years, explained hers away. "When I worked there, I didn't ever actually have anything happen to me," she said. "A couple of times I would know I had a door shut and then I'd go about my business and it would be open." Linda attributes this to the age of the house.

But historical interpreter Phyllis Green, who now works as the schoolmarm at the Mt. Gilead historic site, experienced something in 2004 she couldn't explain. "I went down to give a tour, and I get into the room where all the pictures are, and that's where the phone is," she said. "I'm telling everyone about Zerelda and how she could hold her own with everybody—her picture's right above the telephone—I'm not really complimentary about her. I tell them she's a tough cookie." Two hours later, while preparing for another tour, something in the house made its opinion known. "I walked in and I was just heading to the staff room ... and all of a sudden I see something shoot across the room and go thud, and I thought, 'What would that be? I'm the only one in here.' The mouthpiece of that phone had shot across the room. Folks had peeked inside the curtains waiting for me to open the door [and] they said, 'What was that? We heard a thud.' I told them she's telling me to keep my mouth shut about her when I'm giving a tour. I share that story and you should see people move away from that phone." The telephone, an old wooden wall phone with its earpiece attached by a cord, sits between two rocking chairs in the family room. People have seen Zerelda's chair rocking. Maybe the earpiece was just the closest thing she could grab to throw at Phyllis.

Michelle Pollard, from England, has visited the James Farm numerous times—even volunteering there in 2004—and has seen Zerelda in that chair. In an article prepared for the farm, "When I die, my spirit will fly straight home," Michelle wrote:

> First, as we entered the parlor, my favorite room, I "saw" Zerelda Samuel sitting in her rocker under the telephone.... She wore a black dress with an off-white shawl across her shoulders, and either held a handkerchief or wore a dress with lace at the sleeves. She rocked gently with both feet flat on the carpeted floor and her hand and sleeve were folded on her lap. She bowed her head in welcome, but was gone before I had time to acknowledge it.

Michelle saw another woman, a "solemn, almost mournful" young woman in a light blue dress, but doesn't know who she was. According to Joyce, it must have been someone with strong ties to the James Farm. "The ghosts that are around there are ghosts of people who have been killed there," Joyce said. "And people who have been associated with that farm for a long time. And people who rode in and never rode out. There's just history there, just lots, and lots, and lots of history."

The county bought the dilapidated farmhouse and 36 acres from descendents of the James family in March 1978, repaired the house, and opened it up for tours the next year. And sometimes, when a historical place is brought back to life, pieces of history are brought back too. Carolyn Brennecka, a historical interpreter at the farm for ten years, found that out for herself. "I don't think anybody can work in a place like that that long and not have some feelings," she said.

Carolyn and fellow interpreter Liz Murphy were present for a ghost hunt by a Missouri paranormal group in January 2005. Although Liz didn't experience anything out of the ordinary, Carolyn did. "The biggest thrill for me was when I used the dowsing rod and communicated with some of the people," she said. Those dowsing rods, made from old wire coat hangers, were supposed to move to the left or right when someone questioned the dead. Carolyn, holding her rods like pistols, said her response was exciting. "Frank has been an intriguing person for me," she said. "I went to talk to him first. I was so excited I was getting some responses. I asked him if anyone else was there, if Annie was there, and that type of thing. I guess what made me more convinced was when I took it into the bedroom and asked if Zerelda was there and the response was so much stronger. I felt it wasn't me doing this. It was being done by someone else. We didn't believe in this stuff," she said. "All I can tell you is after that night, I'm more open."

In the house, Liz showed me the phone, Zerelda's rocker, and the stone fireplace where the James family swept the Pinkerton "bombs" to keep them from burning down their home. But as we walked out of the James house, Thomas and Liz stepped off the trail and walked a little northeast of the home. I followed the trail back to the museum because I didn't want to join them for this hunt. Thomas had told Liz his theory of an important piece of James Farm history he hoped to excavate some day—he was trying to scare up the ghost of the James' privy. That's one ghost hunt I can do without.

Jesse James Farm

21216 Jesse James Farm Road, Kearney, MO 64060

Phone: 816/628-6065
Website: www.jessejames.org
Hours: May through September, 9 AM-4 PM daily; October through April, 9 AM-4 PM Monday through Saturday; noon to 4 PM Sunday.

Chapter 26

Governor's Mansion
JEFFERSON CITY

The state capitol dome looms over Jefferson City like a monument from the ancient world. The dome is topped with a statue of the Roman deity Ceres, goddess of grain and agriculture, to celebrate the state's agrarian past, present, and future. I was about twenty minutes early for my appointment at the Governor's Mansion and I hadn't been to the capitol building since a field trip in the fifth grade. All I remember from that trip is the bus stopped at Long John Silver's for lunch—not the only memory of my trip to the state capitol I wanted to have.

This was the third capitol building to be constructed on that spot. The first two were destroyed by fire in 1837 and 1911. This Renaissance-style structure, built in 1918, covers three acres in downtown Jefferson City. The Missouri Museum is located on the first floor, but that's not why I was

there. I trudged up the stairs and into the building, only to find more steps to trudge up. At the top of the stairs I stepped into the rotunda, with its great decorative ball hanging from the inside of the dome, and bronze state seal set into the floor. To my right were the Senate chambers, to my left the House. I walked to the House doors and looked through a window. A group of men and women (mostly men) dressed in more brown than you see in an average day were waving their arms and yelling about something. Good. The legislators were at work instead of entertaining beer lobbyists. Now I could relax and get on with my business.

Down the bluff from the state capitol building is the Jefferson Landing State Historic Site featuring the 1839 Lohman Building, a historic tavern and hotel that serves as a visitor's center, the 1855 Union Hotel, home of the Elizabeth Rozier Gallery, and the Governor's Mansion, which was my destination. I wasn't there to visit the governor. Heck, I didn't even know if he was home. I was there to visit a resident who had been in the mansion a lot longer than the current governor—her father had accepted the surrender of outlaw Frank James in 1882. The three-story, brick, 20,000-square-foot mansion was built in 1871 by St. Louis architect George Ingham Barnett at a price of $75,000. The first residents, Gov. Benjamin Gratz Brown and his wife, Mary Hansome Gunn Brown, moved in January 20, 1872. The mansion has been the home of thirty-three governors and their families, and has hosted guests like the Grand Duke Alexis of Russia, General George Custer, Confederate president Jefferson Davis, British Prime Minister Edward Heath, President Harry Truman, politician William Jennings Bryan, Secretary of State Henry Kissinger, President Bill Clinton, and Vice President Al Gore.

I went to the wrought iron front gate. It was locked. My appointment was at 1:30 PM, and it was 1:30 PM. I hit the intercom buzzer. "Hello," said a voice that was probably attached to a guy with a black suit packing a gun. "How may I help you?" "I had an appointment at 1:30," I said. "Come around to the vehicle entrance," the voice told me.

The vehicle entrance was a large black gate equipped with video cameras—a lot like the gates in movies where rich guys have people like me tossed out. As I approached the gate, it swung open by itself. I walked through, and a man with a black suit approached me. If he was packing, it was subtle. "Come this way," he said and led me inside. There should have been something comforting about being escorted by a bodyguard, except it wasn't my body he was guarding.

Inside I met Mary Pat Abele, executive director of Missouri Mansion Preservation, Inc., in her Governor's Mansion office. Mary Pat has worked in the mansion thirty-one years. "Since I was a baby," she smiled. Mary Pat was organizing the mansion for the children's etiquette event for the next day. When she took me to the ground floor from the staff offices in the basement, I walked through chairs and tables arranged for the young visitors' lessons. The kids were going to learn table manors, table settings, and written and verbal communication. "It's a very active house," Mary Pat said. "All of these things are going on."

Sixty thousand people come through the Governor's Mansion each year—in the spring, sometimes as many as 1,000 people a day. Today, I hadn't seen anyone outside the security and food staff, and they were in the basement. Every part of the mansion open to the public has been restored to a different decade from the 1800s to honor the early days of the mansion. "It's one of the oldest buildings [in the country] built as a governor's residence and it has continued to be used as that," Mary Pat told me. "One hundred thirty-five years."

She led me across the ground floor to a door with a great window facing a courtyard that overlooks Madison Street. The Missouri Children's Fountain, featuring children and Missouri birds and fish, dominated the scene. "At the turn of the century, when the Stephens [Governor Lawrence "Lon" Vest and Margaret "Maggie" Nelson Stephens] were here, they had a fountain," Mary Pat said. "Over the years, it fell into disrepair." The Stephens' cast iron fountain had deteriorated into nothing resembling a fountain by the time Governor Mel and Jean Carnahan lived in the mansion from 1992 to 2000. Mary Pat opened the door and led me outside onto a brick walkway where. ... The door swung shut behind us. There had been no one in the room with us to have shut the door. Mary Pat tried the handle. The door was locked. "We might have to go around the back," she said. I wouldn't normally be suspicious about a door in a 135-year-old building swinging shut by itself—even when there is no wind—but what Mary Pat told me next at least made me curious.

"When the Carnahans were in office, there was interest in rebuilding the fountain," Mary Pat began. "We were looking for someone who could do something with children playing with water and this is the same time we were working on the history of the mansion. We thought Carrie Crittenden, who died of diphtheria, should represent children's health." The representation of Carrie Allen Crittenden, frozen in bronze, forever plays atop the fountain. She was the reason I was at the Governor's Mansion. Carrie is the only child to have died in the mansion. She has been seen around the mansion over the years, but she wasn't carved in bronze. "Carrie Crittenden, who was the daughter of Mr. and Mrs. Crittenden, died in 1882," Mary Pat continued. "It was to Governor Crittenden to whom Frank James surrendered." The nine-year-old "golden-haired" Carrie died of diphtheria on December 20, 1882. She was seen again one hundred years later.

"In 1982, there was a worker in the attic repairing the duct work," Mary Pat said. "He told security, 'You might want to let the governor know his daughter was up in the attic playing.'" Then somebody told him the governor, Christopher "Kit" Bond, didn't have a daughter.

"There'd been a little girl, eight or nine, talking to one of the workers," Mary Pat explained. "The worker turned a palish color, went to lunch, and never came back."

Back in the mansion, Mary Pat took me to the third floor. It was from this floor that first lady Agnes Lee Hadley and her children watched the State Capitol building go up in flames in 1911. The third floor also held the ballroom and the Crittenden room. "Not that we know this is where Carrie died," Mary Pat said, "but the furniture was donated by the Crittenden family." The bedroom furniture was presented to the state by the Crittenden family in November 1937 in memory of Carrie. Carrie isn't the only person who has died in the house: Governor John Sappington Marmaduke died in the mansion on December 28, 1887, and first lady Mary Elizabeth Dockery died there on January 1, 1903. But Carrie is the only spirit who has been reported.

"There's been what some of the first families would call some sightings in the house," Mary Pat said. "When I'm the only one here at night, all of a sudden I'd hear the pipes clanging back and forth and I think, 'What do I need to do now?'" Staff members have heard laughter when no one is around, and the elevator has been known to move between floors for no apparent reason. Because of this, for the past thirteen years, Missouri Mansion Preservation, Inc. has hosted a haunted mansion tour for Halloween. And why not give Carrie some attention? "She's a very friendly ghost," Mary Pat said.

Governor's Mansion

100 Madison Street, Jefferson City, MO 65101

Phone: 573/751-7929
E-mail: mmpi@MissouriMansion.org
Website: www.missourimansion.org
Tours: By appointment only on Tuesdays and Thursdays except during August and December. Twenty-four-hour advanced registration by phone call or e-mail required.

Someone's Watching You

There's a baby crying, but nobody's there. Young lovers parted by death search for one another along the lonely country road. The victim of a frame-up keeps a watchful eye over the place where he was arrested and dragged away in chains. A man tied to a chair in a hotel room is stabbed over and over. But these lost souls, lingering in the places they died, don't sit quietly as the living invade their homes. They make themselves known, sometimes mournfully, sometimes playfully, sometimes violently. Enter peacefully, but always—always—look behind you.

Chapter 27

Old Tavern Restaurant
ARROW ROCK

Cars don't really belong in Arrow Rock, a town of seventy-nine residents off US 41. Neither do the satellite dishes that dot the roofs around town, the rubber-soled shoes that smack against the boardwalk, or the electricity that flows through the buildings. Horses belong in Arrow Rock. Ice cream socials belong in Arrow Rock. Guys wearing muttonchops belong in Arrow Rock. The twenty-first century does not. I drove past the 1872 Christian Church, the newspaper museum, and the antique shops, heading for the Old Tavern Restaurant, where you can get good fried chicken, a tour of the historic business, and maybe a glimpse of something unexpected. A group of people, some with cameras, some with ice cream cones from the little café on the boardwalk, ambled across the street. They may be staying at one of the little town's many bed and breakfasts, or they may have just stopped by for the day. I parked on the street and stepped back into 1850.

Arrow Rock sits on a bluff that once overlooked the busy Missouri River. River traffic brought all sorts of people to Arrow Rock—adventurers,

businessmen, wanderers, and people just looking for a home. The town has been home to three state governors, painter George Caleb Bingham, and Dr. John Sappington, who found the cure for malaria. "Arrow Rock used to be the bustling city on the river," said Kathy Borgman, executive director of Friends of Arrow Rock, Inc., and owner of Borgman's Bed & Breakfast. "But the river changed." So has Arrow Rock. Once a stopping place for travelers west, it's now a destination for people who want to see a Broadway-quality show at the historic Lyceum Theatre, or shop for antiques in one of the many shops, or for those who simply long for a lifestyle that's been lost for generations. Old, thick trees are sprinkled throughout the yards of the little tourist town, offering shade and a place to picnic.

I grabbed a glass of iced tea at the little café on the boardwalk. The old wooden walkway offered a shaded area with benches, a checkerboard table, and a lazy cat. Past a general store, several antique shops, and the café, was the Arrow Rock Information Center, where you can ask questions, buy souvenirs, or just pop in for a shot of air conditioning on a hot day. That day's volunteer, Casey Exendine, a University of Central Missouri history major, smiled when I told her why I was in town. "There is a rumor that the tavern is haunted," she said.

I left the boardwalk and crossed the street to a brick sidewalk running across the front of a two-story brick building. An old sign reading J. Huston Tavern Restaurant hung motionless in the still afternoon air. The 1834 building has been home to a tavern, inn, and mercantile. Now it's owned by the State of Missouri as a historic site and contracted out to Mike and Mary Duncan, who run the Old Tavern Restaurant.

"In-A-Gadda-Da-Vida, honey. Don't you know that I love you … In-A-Gadda-Da-Vida, baby. Don't you know that I'll always be true." Iron Butterfly played on the oldies station as I walked through the banquet room, with its wooden floors and brick fireplace, and found the kitchen. Mike and Mary were cleaning after the lunch crowd had gone.

They don't much believe in ghosts. "I haven't experienced anything," Mike said. "In the early years when I went upstairs, I'd find a little cold spot or something like that." Just a cold spot? But are there ghosts in the Old Tavern? "There's always a possibility," Mary said. "We're not trying to promote it as such, but if people ask, we'll tell them there are some."

But Bunny Thomas knows there are ghosts at the Old Tavern Restaurant—she used to live with them. "There are ghosts there," she said, sitting in the comfort of her new business venture, Bunny's Bed and Breakfast, also in Arrow Rock. Her first experience goes back thirty years to her first few nights as a waitress at the Old Tavern in 1976. "At that time it had swinging doors, and we were getting ready for lunch, and I walked through those doors and a very male, very sexy voice said, 'Hello there,'" she recalled. "And I looked around and no one was there." At the time, nobody working there believed she had heard a disembodied voice. "I talked to Clay [Marsh, then the proprietor] and my daughter. I said, 'Somebody spoke to me,' and they said, 'What are you drinking?' And I hadn't been." They all later found it wasn't unusual to hear your name called by someone invisible. "We all had them call our name," said Clay, manager from 1976 to 1979 and proprietor from 1981 to 1986 and 1993 to 2000. "We would hear stuff all the time—doors slamming, windows shutting—when there was nobody there."

Megan Kennedy, a Missouri State University student, volunteers for Friends of Arrow Rock, and she knows what Bunny and Clay are talking about. "In the summers, we usually open up the windows in the bedrooms," she said. "In the mornings, that was one of my jobs." But in 2003, she decided someone else should probably have that job. "I was in one of the back bedrooms opening up the windows and it's just kind of creaky up here," she explained. "I heard something creak, and I heard [a] door shut. And I thought it was Mary [Duncan]. I came back out and sure enough the door was closed. I went back downstairs, and Mary's not there. There was nobody in the tavern to have shut the door. I hate going in there and opening up the windows anymore. I don't want to go there by myself."

Lynn Jackson has worked at the restaurant for four years. She has also heard her share of noises. "We had a full room, and there was a loud noise, and I went up[stairs] and nothing was moved," she said. "There are just noises and things being moved." Does the restaurant have ghosts? "Yes," Lynn said. "We have."

In the 1980s, when Bunny was going through a divorce, she lived in an apartment above the restaurant and her experiences escalated to more than just disembodied voices and doors shutting. "The very first night I moved in, everybody came down and played cards," she said. "When everybody left and I got undressed and got in bed and I heard the stairs squeaking and I heard the floor squeaking and the next thing I knew, the floor at the foot of my bed was squeaking. And I sat up in bed and there was nobody there. I put a table over that spot after that."

She also kept the radio on to mask any bumps in the night—but that didn't always work. During the winter, when business was slow, Bunny worked at a tavern in nearby Marshall as a cocktail waitress. She usually didn't get home until two in the morning. "I always slept with the radio on so I couldn't hear anything," she said. "But one night, I came home, exhausted, and flopped across the bed and I heard static. I looked [at] the dial on the radio and it was like a kid was moving the dial. I sat up and I thought it was on fire because there was a smoke all around it. It was a ghost. It was just like people described it being. It was wispy and you could see through it. It was just an outline."

But Bunny's upstairs apartment, now the restaurant's office, isn't the only spot people have seen a presence. "The last thing that happened was right before we left," Bunny said. It was 2000, the last year Clay and Bunny ran the restaurant. "We were shutting down. I would always go around and check everything. I walked into the taproom and saw a woman standing there. I thought she was a customer. I went in to tell her I'd let her out and then there was nobody there. She was a large lady dressed in a paisley-type dress. She had a round face. Her hair was pulled back like it was in a bun."

And it's not just Bunny—Clay has also seen the same woman. "I saw the woman one time in the front part of the taproom," he told me. People sensitive to psychic phenomena have sensed a man in the building. And Clay has said he, and others, have seen a man's face that looks a little like his staring out of one of the nine upstairs windows, "third window from the left," he explained.

So who is the woman? Clay said there is a legend associated with her. "When it was a stagecoach stop in the 1840s, a woman traveling alone, which was odd at that time, got a room by herself," he said. "In the middle of the night, the other guests heard a lot of moaning and a baby crying. Nobody thought anything, but the next morning they found bloody spots and bloody footprints down the stairs, through the snow, and to the river. I heard the baby crying on several occasions. I could swear to God it was a baby. It could be God knows what, but it was a baby crying. When the tavern used to house people, they heard a baby."

Much like Megan, Clay has heard doors shut in the tavern when no one was around, but he has also seen something no one else has seen—a cradle rocked by itself in an upstairs bedroom. "When it's dark and you're tired, these things are magnified," Clay said. "It could be psychological, but a lot of these things happened in broad daylight." However, neither Clay nor Bunny ever felt threatened in the tavern. "No, I didn't feel threatened," she said. "But I've heard grown men say you couldn't pay them to go in there after dark."

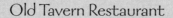

Old Tavern Restaurant

302 Main Street, Arrow Rock, MO 65320

Phone: 660/837-3200
Tours: available through the Friends of Arrow Rock, Inc., 660/837-3231

Chapter 28

Spook Light
Seneca

Hey Spooky! Say Spooky! What are you telling me?
You talk about Spirits, I never did see.
—"Hey Spooky" by Arthur P. "Spooky" Meadows, May 31, 1956

Spook Light Road is dead at dusk. The dusty gravel lane connects Newton County, Missouri, with Oklahoma. Kansas isn't far away; Arkansas isn't either. And people see things here—spooky things. I guess traffic isn't one of them, though a layer of dust that clung to the weeds in the shallow ditches tipped me off that people do use Spook Light Road—sometimes. I pulled my car toward the ditch next to a thick group of trees that would probably seem a little creepy after dark. The trees formed an arch over the road further down, but I wasn't going that far—that would be in Oklahoma. I was in the Ozarks to see the Spook Light, a glowing ball that bounces down the road from rural Oklahoma and onto the hood of your car before suddenly blinking out, only to reappear behind the car like it had gone right through you. I'm told it happens a lot.

Spook Light Road isn't marked. If I didn't know the road was labeled E50, I would have never pulled onto it. The Spook Light is sometimes still called the Hornet Spook Light, but time has rendered the town of Hornet into just a smattering of houses. It was easy to miss too. It was about 7:30 PM when I arrived, so I was going to have to wait awhile to see this mysterious light. It wouldn't be dark until after 8:00 PM, and the Spook Light might not show up until close to midnight. But I had followed directions, so I was in a good spot to see it. "You never know quite where to stop on the road," local historian Virginia Hoare said. "But people say, 'Where do you find the most beer cans? That's where you can stop and see the Spook Light.'"

Virginia has seen the Spook Light, so I trusted her. "When I was in high school, and I graduated in 1934, I saw it," she said. "It came right through the car. We saw it coming toward us, and I looked out the back window and I saw it had passed through the car." That's what I was hoping would happen to me. I had driven through the nearby town of Seneca earlier that day on my way to see the light. The little town of 2,135 nestled in the Ozarks is just south of Joplin. It has a Dollar General Store, a Simple Simon's Pizza, and a Dairy Queen. The Spook Light is nearby, too, but you wouldn't know it by driving through Seneca, though there are plenty of spirits in the liquor stores on the south side of town near the Oklahoma state line. Seneca mayor Gary Roark says he has heard of the Spook Light, but "I've never seen it. But I don't think I've been out there two or three times and one was as an adult. I won't say I'm a skeptic because I know too many people who've seen it."

Cicadas sang in the thick trees along Spook Light Road as dusk turned into night. I had been on the road for about an hour and hadn't seen another vehicle. A dog barked in the distance. At least, I hoped it was a dog.

The Spook Light has a tragic past. Legend has it two Quapaw Indian lovers—chased by warriors and an angry father—jumped to their death into the Spring River from a cliff called the Devil's Promenade. The lovers are the ones walking this lonely little road scaring the bejesus out of drunken teenagers on Saturday nights. Could be. The Spook Light has been around awhile. "The light began appearing when people settled here in 1886," Virginia said, "but the local Indians said it started appearing in the early 1800s." So what is it, really, this yellowish-white, basketball-sized will-o'-the-wisp on the Missouri/Oklahoma state line? A lot of people have tried to find out.

The U.S. Army Corps of Engineers investigated the Spook Light in

1946. "They tried to prove it's the refraction of headlights from a nearby road," Virginia told me. "They couldn't prove this, so they called it 'lights of unknown origin.'" But "unknown origin" isn't good enough for some people, and the speculation continues. "There have been studies by scientists who've tried to find out what it was," Gary said. "The best guess was gasses coming out of the ground. But that doesn't jibe with what people have reported."

Bonnie Horner of Blue Springs was a teenager in Webb City, a small town north of Joplin, during the late 1950s and early 1960s. She has seen the Spook Light at least a dozen times, and she doesn't buy terrestrial explanations. "They say it's headlights, and it's not headlights," she said. "It's a light, but this light stays the same size no matter where you are, whether you're in front of it or behind it." She stopped and smiled. "Maybe God has a disco ball."

It's dark now on Spook Light Road. I notice black shapes in the roadway ahead. I watch them and think they might be moving. Is it the dog I heard earlier? Are they shadows from the trees hanging over the road? Is it Bigfoot? About 9:00 PM a truck drives by. Its headlights reveal the black shapes were just shadows. But wait—I see another light. It's moving, it's bouncing, it's flittering.

Flittering? It's a lightning bug. I sit back and wait some more. Roberta Williams of Carthage, a city about a half-hour drive away from E50, has seen the light before, and it wasn't a bug. "It was before midnight," she said. "It was like a big huge ball. A yellow glow—and it went right straight through our car. I just screamed. All of us looked at each other. We said, 'Let's get out of here.' We weren't even drinking."

At about 10:00 PM I heard gunshots. Not the most comforting sound to hear 200 miles from home on a gravel road in the Ozarks, in the dark. A building that sits at the head of Spook Light Road on the state line used to be a museum. Arthur "Spooky" Meadows owned the place and called it Spooksville. He served food and wrote songs about the Spook Light. He later sold the museum to Garland "Spooky" Middleton, who sold soda to people who stopped by to see the light. "He was kind of a nut," Virginia said.

At precisely 11:14 PM, a bird chirped in the woods to my left. At least I think it was a bird. It sounded like an Indian "strike at my signal" noise from a 1950s Western. I was starting to get a little nervous. What I wouldn't give for a crowd of drunken teenagers to come by so I could tell them to shut the heck up. But nobody was around, not even the police.

"I've never seen it," said Capt. Richard Leavens of the Newton County Sheriff's Department. "I've heard from a lot of people who swear they have. I've been out there several times as a teenager and a few times as an officer and I've never seen anything. But people I would say would be reliable have said it's bounced on the hood of their car." Yeah, people keep saying that. Wait. I see a light. It's the light. It's bouncing up the road. It's ... just a car. The car creeps by at about ten miles an hour with a teenage boy sprawled across the hood grinning like he had just found something neat in a box of Lucky Charms. Great, I had finally seen some drunken teens on Spook Light Road, but still no Spook Light.

Bill Caldwell, librarian for the nearby *Joplin Globe*, hasn't seen the Spook Light either, but he knows why people are interested. "It's such a community happening. It's just part of the landscape," is his explanation. "It is unexplained and intangible, there's just no way to know what it is." And the locals want to keep it that way. It would detract from the mystery. "I'd hate for them to find out what it was," Virginia said.

It was getting late and the owls were making a terrible hooting fuss in the trees. Owls are supposed to be bad omens, aren't they? Maybe hanging out alone on a country road in the middle of nowhere waiting for a ghost light to come dance on the hood of my car wasn't such a great idea. Sometime after midnight, I got tired and left without seeing the Spook Light— but that doesn't mean it doesn't exist. "It's a little bit like people with stories about UFOs," Gary said. "There's no doubt they've seen something, but what it is is anybody's guess."

Yeah, I'll be back.

Spook Light Road

Driving directions: From Joplin, take Interstate 44 to Exit 4 (MO 43). Take MO 43 south 4 miles to Gum Road; turn right. Continue on Gum Road until you reach a T; turn right. Turn right onto E50, which is Spook Light Road. Park next to the biggest pile of empty beer cans and wait.

Chapter 29

Pythian Castle

SPRINGFIELD

Pythian Castle is set back from a mildly busy street in Springfield. The street may have been busier during an earlier time, when U.S. Army vehicles came to and from the castle, but that was sixty years ago. Obscured from the road by its distance and a high chain link fence in what was once a football field of a front yard, the coldly elegant Pythian Castle is one of twenty such castles in the state.

From its long drive, the castle seems to rush at you like an effects shot in a suspense movie. It has hosted weddings, dances, and a murder mystery theater, though, according to Dawn Newlan, a medium with the Ozark Paranormal Society, the people of Springfield hardly know it's there. Which is a darned shame—it is beautiful. The castle, its gray stone exterior looking impervious to trebuchet-fire (or at least angry villagers with torches and pitchforks) was built in 1913. It has housed orphans and widows of the Knights of Pythias fraternal organization, soldiers and German prisoners of war during World War II, and a hospital.

Parking in the small lot in front of the castle, I looked for any signs of movement on the castle's upper floors. Owners Tamara Finocchiaro and her mother, M. J. Page, didn't have to be home for the curtains to move or for shadows to dance across the window. They are not the castle's only residents. Lee Prosser said he is well aware of the castle's haunted reputation. "Be wary of Pythian Castle, it'll touch you," he told me. "When you face it, then you go up the steps and you go to the right and look up, you'll be watched. You'll see. Be prepared. Be prepared for anything."

I looked up to the right and saw nothing in windows darkened by the waning light of the afternoon. That didn't mean, of course, that something wasn't looking back at me. Whatever was in there, it gave Lee enough of a start, he never made it inside the castle. "[I got] close to the [window] panes and it was sufficient," he said. "I got a sense of dread there. It reeked of dread, so I just turned and went off."

I stood at the end of the walk—maybe I shouldn't have spoken to Lee before I went to the castle. Tamara and Dawn met me as I entered Pythian Castle; the tall ceilings of the ground floor made me feel extraordinarily small behind the stone walls. Tamara and M. J. have done a lot of restoration to the once-neglected structure, bringing a good bit of it back to its original beauty. Of course, it took them a while to find the right people to work on the building. "Before we fixed it up we had a bad time finding a contractor," Tamara said. "They'd peel out of here."

Maybe, just maybe, that had something to do with the presence Lee warned me about. Dawn was aware of many presences at the castle, but none made her uncomfortable. "They always meet me at the driveway," Dawn said as we walked to the dining room to sit down and discuss the castle spirits before the tour.

"Who meets you?" Tamara asked.

Dawn smiled as she pointed above her head. "The ones upstairs. They stare at me."

Tamara and M. J. have owned Pythian Castle for about four years, and they know the building is haunted. "I've heard a door slam in the basement," Tamara said. "People have heard things like chains drop. One night at 3:00 AM, our dog stood there barking toward the stairwell. Mom heard stacking noises in the basement like someone was stacking shelves, but there was nobody in the building. Who would have been stacking shelves at 3:00 AM?" The encounters have also gotten a little personal. "When I've been sleeping I've been woken up four times with them," Tamara said. "They used my name. One of my customers swears they call her name."

Tamara, a professional dancer, holds dance classes at the castle. "One of my dance people came running down the stairs sheet white [and] said, 'You're right, he's following me,'" Tamara said. "We get a lot of little orbs flying around and I see things out of the corner of my eye and say, 'Just stop it already.'" Tamara said the spirits that haunt the Pythian are from different times in the castle's varied history. "Some date back to the orphan era, like the one who likes to reside in our theater upstairs. It was his fondest place in the castle," she said. "Some ghosts tend to be in the military period from the 1940s. They don't seem to be as friendly."

Maybe that's because the ghosts from the castle's Army days are stuck in the basement. "People don't like to go in the basement," Tamara told me. "My dog doesn't like going down there. People think military men linger down there and some prisoners of war. You had maybe some bad treatment going on."

Lee said he felt something wrong with the basement during his brief visit too. "There was something horrible happen in the second basement," he said. In the basement, where I would visit soon enough, people have reported seeing an apparition—something rare for the castle.

"People could swear they've seen a person walking," Tamara said. "They could see him, describe what he was wearing, and know his name. It was Jeff."

Dawn has been able to pin down the rough identities of the basement ghosts, but not much more. "As much as we can tell, there are two men and a woman," she explained. "I'm assuming her to be a teacher who was here when it was an orphanage. Both the guys are military. One appears to be casual. Never in uniform. He was in Bermuda shorts, Hawaiian shirt, and flat top. The other one, he has stripes. I don't know if he's a sergeant, but there's more than one stripe on his sleeve. The two I see are American. They're our soldiers." But it's not just mental images or the occasional sighting that convince Tamara and Dawn there is something in the bowels of the castle—it's the voices.

"In the basement, we've heard two or three different voices," Dawn said. "We've actually got voices on tape. Very distinct accents. The ones downstairs will actually interact with you. You can ask questions and they won't necessarily answer you there, but later on tape." Sitting at a table in the vast dining hall, Dawn played some of the EVPs for me that the Ozark Paranormal Society recorded at two different times in 2005. "There are at least five separate entities I have been able to determine," Dawn said. The voice of a man, possibly mad, moaned, "I am not myself" on the first floor. In the basement room where the Army interrogated German POWs, a low voice, like a boot crunching on gravel, growled, "Punish him." In the second floor theater, a slow, plaintive Southern voice drawls, "I'll kill him." Dawn also played indeterminable whispers, a woman's laughter, and the faint sound of a man's voice hissing, "It's okay."

"Each one of the ghost hunting people have gotten something unusual here," Tamara said. "I've heard the EVPs from different groups. They each get voices on tape because they're so clear."

The ghosts of the castle performed well during the last ghost hunting tour of the castle. I hoped when I took my tour after darkness had finally crept over Springfield, they would be on again tonight. Tamara, Dawn and I sat around the dining hall table waiting for the sun to set. Dawn didn't want to start my tour until after dark, but I think they were just trying to see which one would be the first to send me screaming out the door.

"We heard the door slam and what sounded like a man screaming in agony," Dawn said of the last tour.

"I think they were being cliché ghosts for the tour," Tamara said.

"Screaming in agony, chains clanking, moaning," Dawn agreed. "We don't normally have things like that."

Tamara smiled. "They were bored," she said. "Let's go mess with the guests." She turned toward me. "The scariest part is the basement."

"It's not that it's scary," Dawn said. "It's just so intense it makes people uncomfortable."

"The dogs don't like the basement," Tamara told me. "Sometimes they wait upstairs for me."

Another member of the Ozark Paranormal Society, David Cole, and his teenage son, Spencer, were seated nearby; Spencer was at another table and David was in a chair directly behind me. Spencer looked a little nervous. Good. I'm glad I wasn't the only one.

"We have a cold spot that's almost always in the basement. I think it's the schoolteacher," Dawn said. "We used a digital thermometer and it was 25 degrees colder than what it was [in other places]. I think it went from 75 to 53 and it's only for about ten seconds. We heard three different types of male voices there. We heard a metal door shut. It sounded like metal-on-metal." Yeah, I was getting more and more excited the more they told me. And by excited, I mean reluctant.

"They have the tendency to push on my bed," Tamara added. Okay, that would have been enough for me. Tamara and M. J. have plans to turn the castle into a bed and breakfast. I was happy there wasn't a room available for tonight.

Other problems in the basement include fresh batteries suddenly draining during ghost hunts and other equipment failure. "Sometimes you're in an area and your batteries are dead, and when you leave it's fine," Dawn said. "It's real bad downstairs."

Tamara left us in the dining room. She was going out later and didn't need to go on a tour to experience the castle—she lived there. Before we ventured into the basement, Dawn told us the group had to stay together. "First, you can fall down the stairs," she said. "Secondly, you can encounter something." Most of the members of the Ozark Paranormal Society are sensitives, meaning they can sense, hear, and sometimes see ghosts. But knowing something is there isn't always a safeguard against it. "Most of them are not trained when they walk into something who tries to invade you," she explained. "Any ghost in any place at any time, you put yourself in the same place with a spirit, anyone who decided they wanted to do a possession, they can. If you don't know how to defend yourself, they can." Um, yeah, this keeps getting better and better.

"People who haven't experienced that think it's make-believe," Tamara said. "But until you experience something that scares the hell out of you, you don't believe it." David stood from his spot behind us and walked over toward Spencer. Spencer took David's vacated chair.

"I literally have been able to see, hear, smell, taste, touch as far back as I can remember," Dawn said. "I can see them, can hear them, and I can see them over there." She pointed toward the shadows at the back of the dining hall, then out the dining hall toward the stairs where she said the spirits were pacing. Yeah, if the ghosts were there, they had us surrounded. "We're going to have an interesting evening," she said. "I was actually attacked by something that tried to suffocate me once."

During ghost hunts, I've felt cold spots, I've felt the air thicken around me, and I've felt claustrophobic—outdoors—but I've never felt like I was under attack. Oh, great. David stirred in his chair. He said he was coming out of a sudden rush of heat that washed over him, breaking him out in a sweat. Everyone else felt fine. "Just sitting behind you guys. Mercy, I was hurtin'. I was sitting where you were sitting," he said, pointing at Spencer, "and I had to move." Spencer's eyes grew wide and he moved too.

Jingles, like crystal wind chimes, tinkled quietly in the corner of the dining room where Dawn said a ghost was pacing. "That noise doesn't belong in the castle," she said. I heard it. David and Spencer didn't. Cool. "It is very active," Dawn said of the castle. "I get a little cranky at Tamara because Tamara has never experienced anything negative. There is especially one, which is very strong, and if it got angry, he could disassemble the place. It's not mean, but when he's irritated, he's irritated."

With that, we went into the basement. Jennifer Kettler, managing editor of the *Fayette Advertiser/Democrat Leader*, researched the Pythian Castle for a story in 2004. She had already warned me about going downstairs. "When we were in the basement, we heard a door slam from the area we were just in," Jennifer said. "That was a little creepy."

Yes, I thought as we descended into the basement, yes it is. Concrete stairs led into a vast system of rooms under the castle. Old furniture and woodworking supplies are stacked at odd spots on many of the walls. Mats line the floor of a long, wide room Tamara uses to practice dance, though her dog, Digby, won't join her. One room holds a great, cast iron boiler with the company name "Spencer" embossed on a door. Spencer didn't appreciate the coincidence. A dark, jagged hole in the boiler room revealed a tunnel that joins the castle to an outbuilding that used to house the military laundry. A mist has been known to form in that tunnel if someone invades the territory of whatever is in there. Dawn seemed surprised the mist didn't form for me.

Some rooms are dank, some dry, and others oddly still in the early night, but none seem to make me uncomfortable. Everyone who warned me I would experience something otherworldly in the castle was, so far, wrong. I tried not to get cocky. In one room, bullet holes dotted the wall like cellulite. The military ghosts have been sensed here. David took digital pictures in this room and others throughout the basement, but few orbs showed up in images. Even those were faint and, to me, quite possibly explainable.

Dawn smiled as she took us through a concrete doorway and into a room that was noticeably stuffier than the others. A dark rectangle sat in a wall of that room—it led to the interrogation room. Dawn flipped on the wall switch and revealed blank concrete walls surrounding a lone chair in the center of the room. This is where soldiers questioned—quite possibly harshly—German POWs. This is also the room where Dawn's EVP growled, "Punish him." Screams would die in this room, I thought, muffled by the mass of concrete. I stood outside the room and snapped a few pictures.

David stepped in, but wasn't in long. "I had to get out of there," he said once we were well away from the room. "That gave me a heck of a headache."

The interrogation room was the epicenter for bad things in the basement. I didn't feel anything bad about the room but, then again, I didn't go in. With that, we went upstairs. Not much paranormal happens on the ground floor, Dawn said. M. J. and the dogs, Princess, Zora, and Digby, lounged in the front room watching television. The dogs were a little calmer than me ... or Spencer.

Then we mounted the steps and went to the second floor theater. The theater on the second floor was one of the first movie theaters in Missouri. Tamara and M. J. have already remodeled this floor and rent it out for weddings and dance recitals. But there is a catch—there's always an extra member of the audience. Dawn took me to a spot next to a wall near the small stage. A large window was open and a cool breeze blew by my head. "He likes to stand here and watch," she said.

Oh, terrific. But Theater Ghost (as Tamara and Dawn call him) doesn't normally cause trouble. "Theater Ghost, on occasion, while he's mostly nice, can be threatening," Tamara said. Although he has never threatened her, Tamara has had more than a passing feeling about him. "I was walking through a plastic drape we hang up and bumped into what I thought was a person behind the drape," she said. "So much so I apologized but nobody was occupying that space. I felt kind of silly."

Theater Ghost is the most powerful ghost in the castle and, according to Tamara and Dawn, there is a reason he can be threatening. "Apparently he was supposedly killed for someone else's crime back in the day," Tamara told me. "One day a guy [was here] who looked like the man who committed the crime, [and the ghost] threatened to kill him. And the man felt shoved while he was in the building."

Dawn was leading a ghost tour that night. "The night we had the guy who was rude. When he was shoved, I was downstairs," she said. The man had been in the theater when he suddenly ran down the stairs screaming for Dawn. "He said, 'Dawn, it's mad, it's mad.'" He had been taunting Theater Ghost. "He was screaming at it, 'Show yourself. Show yourself,'" Dawn said. "Me and another person walked into the theater. I walked in and was first hit with the anger. I could feel the entity say, 'There he is, there he is.'" But who was 'he'?

Dawn said there have been rumors of child abuse when the castle was an orphanage. One was the rumor of a girl being beaten, raped, and killed. Theater Ghost, she said, was the one blamed for it. "I felt he was a large black man volunteering here out of the kindness of his heart," she said of the impressions she received from the ghost that night. "I saw three men in uniform. I don't know what they were. And they tell whoever they know this is the guy who beat and raped this girl, but one of the three men was actually the one who did it." She said Theater Ghost is convinced the man he pushed is the reincarnation of the man who raped and killed the girl. "The entity upstairs is positive that's the guy. He really does not like the one guy."

Standing by the open window, the breeze still hitting my back, I noticed my arms and face had grown hot. But it wasn't from the temperature in the room. The rest of my body was comfortable, but my face and arms felt like I was standing too close to a stove. "He's very powerful," Dawn warned. "You know how I told you he could tear down this whole castle? He could. His energy is that strong." My head grew light and my face was uncomfortably hot, so I left the room. "The theater is the most intense spot in the castle," Dawn said. "Apart from the interrogation room." Standing in the theater lobby for a few minutes, I felt fine. Jennifer had told me about the second floor too. When she visited the castle, she found what she was looking for there.

"We had gone to the second floor and we were right in the lobby area of the old movie theater," Jennifer said. "This is a really open lobby area and people would gather there before the movie. We stayed up there for quite some time. We just sat in the lobby area and talked, and I just stood up away from the group, and snapped a series of pictures. Five different pictures in a matter of seconds. I really wanted to get a ghost on film. Ooh. Here's going to be the proof if anything."

When she finished the interview, she went back to her office and pored through the photographs. "When I'd taken the five shots in the foyer, the first shot, there's nothing in the photo," she said. "In the second shot, there's a few orbs. In the third shot it's full of tons of orbs. The fourth had fewer, and the fifth was empty. I don't know what happened in that sequence, but something happened." The orbs may have congregated there because the lobby was a gathering spot back in the castle's theater days. Why not? "I feel my experience at the castle was legitimate because I was skeptical," she said. "When I saw those pictures I thought, this is proof. Seeing is believing."

Most of the third floor of the castle is unfinished. Rooms with torn hardwood floors and doors with Army stencils dominate. A large room on the third floor was filled with scaffolding. It was to be turned into a bed and breakfast suite. The castle was going to be even more beautiful once it was finished. But it was late, we were out of rooms, and the ghosts were being uncooperative. The five of us left at 11:00 PM, but as we walked down the outside stairs to the parking lot, we silently turned and took one last look at the castle. One window on the third floor to the right seemed to pull my attention toward it. That was the future bed and breakfast suite.

"There's something moving up there," Dawn said nodding toward the window I was drawn to. Yeah, Lee was right, I think I was being watched.

Pythian Castle

1451 East Pythian Street, Springfield, MO 65802

Phone: 417/865-1464
E-mail: tamara@pythiancastle.com
Website: www.pythiancastle.com
Tours: 5:30 PM Tuesdays and Thursdays, 3:30 PM Saturdays
Admission: adults $5; children 6-12 $2.50; children under 6 free.

Landers Theatre

SPRINGFIELD

Laughing stone faces stare onto the street from the front of the Landers Theatre in old downtown Springfield. The four-story theater sits among street
after street of historic buildings that are now home to art galleries, restaurants, and coffee shops. There may be food, coffee, and occasionally art in
the Landers, but it's a theater. It's always been a theater. The building was
constructed in 1909 by John and D. J. Landers and R. W. Steward and has
been in continuous use as a movie or stage theater since its opening act, *The
Golden Girl,* in September

1909. The Landers, which is
on the National Register of
Historic Places, is home to
the Springfield Little Theatre company. When the
theater was young, the area
may have been painted with
bootleggers and ritzy hotels,
but it is now part of a com-
puter-friendly arts district,
where banners hanging
from lampposts proclaim
the area a wireless Internet
zone. I tried the wireless Internet as I sat across from
the theater, waiting for a
Butternut truck to move so I
could get a really good look
at the building. The loading
zone in front of the theater
is popular with delivery

trucks. After carting bread to several restaurants on the block, the driver stopped into an ice cream shop. I had plenty of time to surf the Internet. After the driver got his scoop of vanilla in a sugar cone and drove off, I got a better look.

The building, with its brick and terra cotta façade, looked much the same as it must have the day it opened—only the plays have changed. Early twentieth century audiences probably wouldn't take well to a production of *The Full Monty*. At least, not respectable audiences. I walked to the side of the building and went down an alley. The Little Theatre business office is accessible through a gangster movie-like brick alley, which helped set the mood for the day. An almost 100-year-old building, a gangster alley, and the occasional plaintive cry of a baby who died in the theater in 1919 add up to an interesting visit. Annie Carlyn, director of marketing and special events for the Springfield Little Theatre, met me in an office dotted with posters for the musicals *Godspell, The Wizard of Oz,* and *Joseph and His Amazing Technicolor Dreamcoat*. She said ghost hunting groups often come to the theater to look for the ghost of the baby and the ghost of a stagehand who allegedly committed suicide. "Groups come in regularly with temperature gauges and cameras and electric impulse sensing equipment," Annie said. "But I've personally never seen a ghost." Annie also doesn't put much faith in the stagehand story. "I've heard several variations that a stagehand committed suicide of one form or another. I don't think any of that is true."

The Landers was one of the centers of entertainment in the region in the 1920s when it joined the Orpheum theater chain. Actors and musicians like John Philip Sousa, Lillian Russell, and Fanny Brice performed at the Landers. The theater still hosts the Springfield Ballet, Springfield Regional Opera, and the Springfield Symphony Chamber Series. "When it opened, it was one of the most lavish theaters," Annie said. Vaudeville was popular at the Landers until an invention by Thomas Edison spread across the country and replaced vaudeville as America's principle form of entertainment. "Movie theaters tolled the death knell of the vaudeville performances," she explained. "It became a theater and went into disrepair."

The Springfield Little Theatre group, which was formed in 1934 and had performed in venues like high schools and churches, eventually bought the theater in 1970. Annie told me, "It has been in the process of restoration ever since." The Little Theatre has worked to return the Landers to its appearance in the year 1909. This year, they replaced the seats. Although the early history of the Landers Theatre was marked by the racial prejudices of the times, it was one of the first public entertainment venues in southern Missouri open to African-Americans. "Originally, the theater was segregated," Annie said. "The second balcony was the seating area for blacks. There was a fire in the building in the late teens and there was one story about a baby on the second balcony who got crushed by the rush to get out of the building because of the fire."

I found my way to the second balcony, which afforded an awkward view of the stage. There were a couple of small exits from the area, a Miller Lite bottle sitting on a box in the middle of one exit. The seats were gone from the balcony, and the space was being used for storage. The balcony was steep, really steep. During a fire, it must have been a clumsy rush of people trying to get out of the building. Chuck Rogers, scenic designer and technical director for the Little Theatre, worked there from 1983 to 2000 and from 2004 until now. He's lived at the Landers Theatre and is familiar with noises on the second balcony.

"The fire was in 1919," he told me. "It gutted the backstage all the way to the brick. It closed for two years and opened as a movie theater. Sometimes when you're up here, you can hear what sounds like footsteps. I've heard that." He has also heard the baby. "Up in the second balcony, you hear a mother and the baby and the baby's crying. I rationalize it. Cats get in here all the time. But there are a lot of noises a one-hundred-year-old theater can make." Standing on the balcony, I felt a little dizzy. Not that I'm afraid of heights, I just felt, well, wobbly. I made sure I stood away from the edge. Medium Dawn Newlan has felt uncomfortable on the second balcony of the theater too. "When I got to the middle of that walk, I literally felt someone was going to push me off," Dawn said. "I heard a baby cry. There's a strong presence there." But she said she didn't know about the baby before she heard it. "I try not to know the history of a place when I go, so it doesn't cloud what I see."

Chuck saw something in the theater around 1997 or 1998—something he still can't explain. "There used to be the women's bathroom here," he said, pointing through a door on the stage level. "This area here was stairs going down. One night I was down doing laundry. About a quarter to eleven I came out and there was a guy standing in front of that piano." The dark brown piano sits in the center of the area where patrons enter the theater and split to the left or right toward their seats. Chuck walked toward the area, motioning like an angry football coach. "He was mid-late 50s, shoulder-length salt-and-pepper hair," Chuck said. "Hawkish nose, bushy eyebrows. He had on blue jeans, boots, sheepskin vest. I was surprised to see someone there." The man gave Chuck little notice. "I immediately thought it was a street person. I said, 'Excuse me. Can I help you?' He just looked at me." The man didn't move. "I said, 'The building's closed.' I started walking toward him. He walked in the opposite direction and looked at me. That started to make me angry." Chuck advanced, but not too fast. "I said, 'Excuse me, you're not supposed to be here.' He walked down into the auditorium, and that really made me mad. I followed him and he'd disappeared." It was the disappearing that bothered Chuck. Chuck called a friend he thought would believe his story, but he didn't tell her what had happened. He just asked her to bring a Ouija board. "I didn't tell her anything," Chuck said. "Pretty much with her Ouija board, she described what I'd seen without me telling her. The Ouija board told her his name was Ned and he used to be an employee at the the-

ater. At that moment in time, I met someone. It was as if you and I were standing here. It was just that apparent. It was a human being standing there. This thing with Ned, I don't believe it or disbelieve it. It's just something I can't explain."

Chuck's other encounter at the theater wasn't so human. "There's what used to be an apartment on the third floor," he said. "For many years the Landers kept it available for staff. I lived there eight years." One night in the late 1980s, Chuck had an unwelcome visitor in his apartment, an apartment lined with windows that overlook the street. "I was asleep in the apartment and something woke me up," he said. "I woke up and normally you can see everything on the street. The buildings, the street lights. But I woke up, and I couldn't see anything." Then he saw why. "I looked in the doorway and there was a shape there. A black kind of shape you couldn't see through. I kind of shook my head and blinked my eyes and it was gone."

Theaters and the paranormal have always been well acquainted. "Historical theaters are all based upon superstition," Chuck said. "When they were building theaters, they would build things into them to protect it from spirits. Like horseshoes." Chuck pointed out golden goblin masks that were mounted on the wall over the theater's box seats. "They're there to scare off all the spirits that may be here," he explained. Does that work at the Landers? Maybe not. Gary Bancroft was cleaning gum off seats when I walked through the theater area. He's heard a few things in the theater, but he is not sure if the sounds are supernatural.

"I was here Sunday and the toilet went off," Gary recalled. "I've wondered if there's a ghost in there, but I haven't encountered one here yet. I haven't experienced anything but that toilet. But they say it happens all the time." He paused and smiled. "Must be a woman ghost." I walked into the bathroom before I left. All the toilets were auto-flush. Sure, yeah, those toilets can go off … if something walks in front of them. None of this paranormal talk bothers Chuck. The normal does. "I'm never scared here," he said. "I'm afraid of reality—vandals. You'd hear people coming down the stairs at three o'clock in the morning and I'd grab a baseball bat or my golf club." The building is beautiful and has to be a great place to see a play. One of the things that makes it beautiful is its history, which also lends to its legend. "There's just so much history in this building," Chuck said. "There can't help but be something supernatural here."

Springfield Little Theatre

311 East Walnut Avenue, Springfield, MO 65806

Phone: 417/869-3869
Website: www.springfieldlittletheatre.org

Chapter 31

Hotel Savoy

KANSAS CITY

Dust and bits of plaster cover the floors of the east wing of Hotel Savoy. In the few unlocked rooms on the seventh floor lie the physical ghosts of the hotel's glory days. Ancient furniture sits broken. In one room, sinks are stacked across the floor like awkward dominoes. In another room, a claw-foot bathtub sits alone. And dust. Everywhere there's dust. The occasional opaque, dirty mirror with green specks of age deep within the glass still hangs on a wall. Word has it some guests in the hotel have seen people in the mirrors. But the people in the mirrors aren't a reflection, because the people aren't really there. "Sometimes they see a face in the mirror brushing their hair," said John Rivera, a busperson who has worked the breakfast shift at the hotel since 1998. He has heard the tales of ghosts from guests at the hotel.

There were old mirrors in almost every room I went into on the east wing. I looked in all of the mirrors I found and saw no one but me. It's a good thing too. The hotel was full of employees and I would hate for someone to hear me scream. The downstairs and

two sections of the Savoy have been remodeled over the years; the east wing is still awaiting rebirth to the past glory of the 116-year-old hotel. It looks like a good place for ghosts, but… "I've been here ten years and I've never experienced anything," said Larry Green, General Manager. "We've had people come in who've heard stories and are disappointed. They were expecting something to happen." Some people, however, haven't been disappointed by the Savoy's spirits.

"A lady from Germany came over here one time and she said she was psychic," Rivera told me as he set tables for breakfast. "We went to the second floor. She was feeling the walls and she said, 'Oh, my God.' She stopped and she got really sweaty. She said, 'I saw a guy tied to a chair and a set of hands stabbing him,'" Rivera said, stabbing at the air with clenched fists. At breakfast, Rivera is often the first hotel employee guests see. They tell him of room lights that flicker, invisible hands that touch them in the night, and moving shadows. "These people don't know each other and they experience the same phenomenon," Rivera said.

Busperson Erin KcKinley hears these stories, too, but she's not too convinced the hotel's haunted. "I had one," McKinley said to Rivera as she helped set tables for the lunch crowd. "I had a lady who said she woke up at three in the morning. She heard a room service cart. She got up and looked down the hall and didn't see anything. Every time she went back to bed she heard it, but it was never there."

I hadn't seen or heard anything as I walked the floors of the Savoy, starting at the top and going through each floor before venturing down to the next—until I reached the fourth floor. It looked like the fifth, sixth, and seventh did before it. Dusty, dark, and deserted. But as I stepped out of the stairwell and began walking down the hall, the air seemed different—thicker, denser, hotter. I snapped a few pictures and peered into a few empty rooms, but it became more difficult to breathe, my breath now coming in short, hard bursts. Something was wrong. Was I being watched? No one was there. Goosebumps sprang on my arms, even though I was sweating in the heavy air. The silence pressed at my eardrums, like I was listening to a seashell the size of a Frigidaire. Panic pulled my chest uncomfortably tight. I turned and hurried down the stairs. By the time I stepped onto the third floor landing, I felt fine. I didn't know until later, but I may have just met a "permanent" resident of the hotel's fourth floor—a child who obviously didn't want me around. "Guests have seen a little girl with a long flowing dress," Rivera said. "She just stands and stares."

And incites panic?

Waiter Curtis Hough, who has worked at the Hotel Savoy for two different periods totaling a little more than a decade, has seen her on the stairs between the fourth and fifth floors. "In 1990, they started the restoration of the hotel," Hough said. "In the bed and breakfast rooms, I thought I saw a little girl about age ten in a long dress—Victorian style—up on the fourth floor. I came down and asked anyone if they should get their kid from upstairs and they said there were no kids on the premises. I thought it was just a joke, but maybe I did see one." Other restless spirits reportedly include a bearded man in a purple jacket wandering the basement, a spirit named Henry in the northwest penthouse, and the ghost of a former manager who died in 1990, Hough said. But none of the spirits seems malevolent—quite the opposite. "This gentlemen from Canada would stay in 545 and every once in a while, when he was concerned about work, a young lady in her mid-20s would put her hands on him and would relax him," Hough said.

Then there is room 505. Legend has it a woman died in room 505's bathtub. Visitors have said the shower curtain shuts by itself and the water comes on. But Mike Dobbins, who lived in 505 since the room was made into one of eight apartments at the hotel, hasn't had an encounter with the shower specter. "I haven't seen anything," he stated. "I haven't heard anything. I had someone who'd come in here and said she'd sensed something, but I'm not in tune with that sort of thing." Green says a lot of the hotel's ghost stories are just that—stories. "I think there was a previous manager that started some of these things and it ended up in a book and the Internet and it kind of snowballed. That's how a lot of legends get started."

Because of the restoration project, parts of the hotel sit empty. More restless spirits may yet show themselves. "I have a feeling that once the hotel is completed," Hough said, "there may be more that come out." Until then, ghost seekers will have to check in and cross their fingers. October, Rivera said, is a popular month. "At Halloween there's a lot of people here," he said. "A lot of weird people."

Hotel Savoy

219 West 9th Street, Kansas City, MO 64105

Phone: 816/842-3575 (toll free 809/728-6922)
Website: www.savoyhotel.net

Chapter 32

Main Street Café
MARCELINE

Downtown Marceline on a Sunday afternoon was quiet. A few cars drove by as families gathered at Ripley Park off Marceline's Main Street USA for a reunion. Happy people in white shirts carried covered dishes of baked beans and potato salad to the gathering by the park's old black train engine. It was like being in Andy Taylor's Mayberry or Beaver Cleaver's Mayfield or maybe even Disneyland. Walt Disney lived in Marceline until he was five. A museum there is named after him, so is a school, and people say that Marceline's Main Street was his model for Disneyland's Main Street USA. But Marceline's old-

est resident was gone before Walt's family came to town. More people met and hugged by the train engine that defines this town. Marceline was founded by the Atchison, Topeka & Santa Fe Railway in 1888. Early Marceline thrived through the railroad, and they say the railroad is responsible for the ghost who has taken up residence in a Main Street USA restaurant since the late 1800s. Locals call her the Lady in White.

"What I understand, she was pregnant, killed

by a railroader, and shoved down a well," said Bruce Matejobsky, who owned the restaurant until late summer of 2005. And he should know—the restaurant is on top of that well. "Supposedly, anyone who worked for the railroad who saw her died sometime soon. But I've never heard of anybody getting hurt. I've got railroaders who come in here every month for meetings and I never hear any of them complaining." I wasn't expecting to see the Lady in White when I walked into the café at 2:00 on a mid-summer Sunday afternoon, happy I'd never worked for the railroad. I didn't expect to see breaded tenderloin on the lunch buffet either, but I did, so I guess anything was possible.

The restaurant closed in 2005, reopened as Zack's Café and Steakhouse, and has since closed again. When I visited, it was the Main Street Café and ketchup and mustard bottles decorated every checker-clothed tabletop of the little restaurant, just like I was used to seeing in the Midwest. The restaurant didn't feel haunted, but places rarely do with sunlight pouring through big, plate glass windows. But something ghostly is here. Former waitress Geraldine Burris is sure of it. "I did see her a few times and I felt her presence more than once," she said. "Definitely, she's there." Geraldine worked at the cafe off and on from 1969 to 1976, and again from the early 1980s until 2001 when she retired. "One morning in particular I had gone in early," she began. "I walked in and flipped on the automatic coffee maker and walked back to the stove to make biscuits and gravy and I thought, 'Oh I hadn't turned on the coffee pot,' and I walked up and saw someone. I saw someone in white." The "someone in white" wasn't at the coffee pot when Geraldine got there.

And Geraldine isn't the only waitress who has seen the Lady. Lisa Lopez from Chicago moved to Marceline with her fiancé, Marceline High School graduate Ryan Straub. Ryan is a ghost hunter, and when Lisa wanted a job, he suggested the café. Ryan investigated the Lady in White while he was in high school and knows there is something to the stories. "It is very active," he said of the café once known as The Hole in the Wall. "There is a lot of activity in that place. I think [the Lady] has an affinity toward waitresses because she was one." Lisa only worked at the Main Street Café from October to December 2004, but those three months were … interesting. "Nothing really happened at first," Lisa said. "But once I got pregnant, that's when things began happening." Lisa and Ryan learned she was pregnant Halloween night. "Little things started happening," she said. "I'd be pouring water glasses and the glasses would shake and hit off each other. I'd look back [in the banquet room] and there were no lights on and I'd turn back around and the light would be on. Then things started to get a little bit more intense."

'Intense' meaning spills would be cleaned up when no one was there to clean them, towels would be folded when no one was there to fold them, and the glasses were, well, they were jiggly. Then in December, the activity became more personal. "I was in the bathroom and I was having some complications with the pregnancy," she said. "I was washing my hands and I looked in the mirror and there was a white young woman figure behind me and I was a little scared and I turned around and no one was there. I saw a younger figure with a white gown on. I think it was because she was pregnant when she was murdered." Lisa didn't stay at the restaurant long after that. "I never really told anybody about it because I wasn't like a strong believer until that happened," she said. "After that I quit because everything got normal with the pregnancy and I moved back to Chicago."

Bruce sat across the table from me, his tattooed arms resting on the tablecloth, a pot of coffee sitting between us. He has owned the restaurant for three years and never saw the Lady in White. But that's not to say he didn't believe in her. "You can say that," he said. "When we first started working on this place, a lot of shit happened." Like items disappearing after they had been put down, things falling for no apparent reason, and then there's the coin. "Right after we first opened up, we went gangbusters for a while," Bruce explained. "Then we slowed down and I was bitching about being broke, and I find an old one-dollar coin on the floor and I have no idea how it got there. We vacuumed and I walked by that spot and never noticed it." But it wasn't just finding the coin that bothered Bruce, the type of coin bothered him. "It was an old Liberty dollar," he said. "If it was a Kennedy it would be different, but it was an old Liberty." The seated Liberty dollar was minted between 1866 and 1873.

Ryan didn't find antique money when he investigated the café, but something did fly through the air. "It started off kind of slow, just like any other investigation," he said. "But as the night went on, it started picking up quite a bit." Lights came on, a cooler next to the basement trapdoor started vibrating like someone was trying to get out, and kitchenware started behaving like kitchenware shouldn't in a Newtonian universe. "The plates, they rattled like crazy," Ryan said. "We had a couple that flew off the table and broke."

Geraldine said the Lady in White had a habit of throwing things, like when Geraldine would clean the kitchen. "I'd think I need to get the towel, and I'd turn around and it was flying to me like someone had thrown it," she said. "I got very used to it; I was never frightened." Bruce got used to the Lady too. She never threw anything at him, but she would call his name. "If you're distracted and something's on the stove burning, you hear your name called and you turn around to find it burning," said Bruce, who also experienced cold spots and odd smells in the restaurant. "I say hello to her in the morning and say good-bye to her at night. We got along good."

Geraldine thinks the Lady sticks around because she feels comfortable in the place she died. "Some people like to think when we die our spirit likes to stay where we've been. I don't know how true that is. Nobody's ever come back to tell me," Geraldine said. "But she must have liked it there, until she was murdered." I left the Main Street Café a little buzzed from all the coffee. The day was still bright, people at the family reunion were picking through the remains of Jell-O desserts, and the Lady in White would probably later pay a visit to someone who wasn't looking for her. "It's all the truth," Geraldine said. "I have experienced it. She's definitely present there and she's a very friendly presence." But it's not like Bruce minded the Lady keeping her distance. "I saw a haunting program and some people got scratch marks," Bruce said. "If that happens, I'm out of here. I'll stand and fight, but I'll be damned if I do it with someone I can't see."

Main Street Café (Zack's Café and Steakhouse)

116 South Kansas Avenue, Marceline, MO 64658

currently closed

Afterword: Belief

Over the past year, I've driven thousands of miles around the state of Missouri, spoken with hundreds of eyewitnesses of paranormal events, and walked through dozens of cemeteries, Victorian mansions, and Civil War battlefields. Each of these spots is unique, but they do have one thing in common—all have had their own periods of violent history. A history so violent it may have bled into the present. Throughout my investigations of haunted places, homeowners, tour guides, and psychics have all asked me the same question: do I believe in ghosts? That's a toughie. Yes, I've felt cold spots, I've heard footsteps, and I've seen a transparent boy. But do I believe?

Belief is a tricky concept. We never know what someone truly believes; only what they *say* they believe. Belief also implies faith, and once faith is involved, the believer no longer needs proof. Without proof, you might never convince anyone else something exists. Just ask all those people who hunt Bigfoot. I need proof. That is why I traveled the state to find things out for myself. In the Lemp Mansion and Yeater Hall, I experienced spots that were at least 20 degrees lower than the surrounding air. Anything strange with that? Yeah, each place was over 90 degrees and had no air conditioning.

At the Grand Avenue Bed and Breakfast I smelled cigar smoke in an area at the end of the walk. Not two steps back from the end, not in the grass on either side of the end, and not out on the city sidewalk—just at the end of the walk. The former owner liked to stand out there and smoke cigars. At Pythian Castle, I spent a few minutes in a "haunted" room; my legs were cold, but my arms and face felt fevered in front of an opened window that brought a breeze into the room. In the Hotel Savoy and Workman Chapel Cemetery, I felt something in the air oppressive enough to drive me away. And these were the only two places I was able to capture an orb on film. Can I explain these things? No. But I won't say they *can't* be explained.

Most of the people I interviewed for *Haunted Missouri* were convinced ghosts exist. And listening to their encounters, I can't say they're wrong or that their accounts differ from others. But do I believe in ghosts? I don't know. Could a 101-year-old building make noises that sound like footsteps? Yes. Could the sound of moaning or a baby crying simply be a cat? Sure. Could items falling off a shelf be caused by something as simple as gravity? Yeah. But can a light switch flip on by itself like it did for me in

Yeater Hall? No. Not possible. Let's just say I accept the possibility that ghosts walk among us. And as long as they don't flip off any switch while I'm around, I'll be hap…

Illustrations

All photography by author, unless otherwise noted.

About Jason

Jason Offutt is an author, a journalism instructor at Northwest Missouri State University, a syndicated humor and paranormal columnist, and not a snappy dresser at all. Jason has been a newspaper editor, general assignment reporter, photographer, newspaper consultant, bartender, farm hand, and the mayor of a small midwestern town. His published work includes the humor books *On Being Dad* and *A Small Town*. He's married to Kimberly Offutt and they live in Maryville, Missouri.

Jason has four children—Tawney, seventeen, Hayden, ten, two-year-old Sam, and the baby. The baby likes to sleep and poop. Sam likes to eat, play at the park, and flirt with waitresses. Tawney likes baseball and music. Hayden likes to pretend he's a superhero—and so does Jason.

In his spare time, Jason hunts ghosts, complains there's nothing on TV, and he likes beer—a lot. You can reach Jason through his Website at www.jasonoffutt.com, or talk to anyone from his hometown of Orrick, Missouri. They know his ma.